C0-FPY-606

Reinventing the People's Library

Greg Gaut

Reinventing the People's Library

Greg Gaut

Reinventing the People's Library
by Greg Gaut

Copyright ©2019, Greg Gaut. All rights reserved. No part of this book may be used or reproduced in any manner whatsoever without written permission except in the case of brief quotations embodied in critical articles and reviews.

Publishing coordination and design by Wendy J. Johnson of Elder Eye Press (www.ElderEye.com) – a design and concierge publishing house dedicated to designing with the best design practices for legibility and clarity, to benefit all eyes, of all ages.

Gaut, Greg

Reinventing the People's Library / by Greg Gaut

First Edition, 2019

ISBN: 9781095283479 (alk. paper)

LCCN: 2019940502

East Side Freedom Library

East Side Freedom Library
1105 Greenbrier Street
St. Paul, MN 55106, USA

www.eastsidefreedomlibrary.org

This publication was made possible in part by the people of Minnesota through a grant funded by an appropriation to the Minnesota Historical Society from the Minnesota Arts and Cultural Heritage Fund. Any views, findings, opinions, conclusions or recommendations expressed in this publication are those of the authors and do not necessarily represent those of the State of Minnesota, the Minnesota Historical Society, or the Minnesota Historic Resources Advisory Committee.

CLEAN WATER LAND & LEGACY AMENDMENT

Manufactured in the United States of America by the KDP Independent Publishing Platform.

Contents

- Introduction -

Our Free Spaces

We can take pride that every town of a certain size in our country has a public library. Big cities have a downtown library which anchors a system of branch libraries spread through the neighborhoods. These libraries are tax-supported public institutions and their services are free to all. They are "free spaces" where everyone from a homeless veteran to a "one percenter" is equally welcome to spend the day. They are also "free spaces" in the sense of being classrooms of democracy—places where the skills and habits of participatory community membership can be practiced. There have been libraries since ancient times, but the public library which reaches out and serves every citizen is a uniquely American invention. Traditionally, libraries had been warehouses for books. Our libraries today are first and foremost places for people.

We live in a time when all public goods are under attack. The commons—those things that we own collectively and can access freely or at very low cost—are shrinking, and with it our sense of community and interconnectedness. A powerful ideology of individual greed and corporate power has taken hold in its place. It pushes the idea that everything of value should be treated as a commodity, something to be bought and sold in the world marketplace. According to this ideology, commerce should be deregulated, public investment curtailed, and public goods turned over to private corporations.

Recent elections have brought champions of this ideology, sometimes called "market fundamentalism" or "neoliberalism," into positions of great power. There is a national movement to privatize or reduce funding for public schools, public parks, public transit, and social welfare programs like Social Security, Medicare, and Medicaid. Even public libraries are threatened.

From a neoliberal point of view, public libraries make no sense. They are, after all, based on sharing and cooperation. They are fundamentally committed to serving everyone without charge. As sociologist Eric Klinenberg argues, libraries are a crucial part of our "social infrastructure," the physical places that allow bonds of mutual respect and collaboration to develop between neighbors of different backgrounds. He includes schools, playgrounds, athletic fields, community gardens, churches, community organizations, farmers markets, and if they are welcoming, even coffeehouses, barbershops and bookstores. But libraries, he says, are "the one place that has consistently promoted a modern ideal of mutual respect and enlightenment."[1] Not surprisingly, they are perhaps our most popular public institution. According to the most recent count, there are 16,568 public library buildings in our country, and although Starbucks and McDonald's seem to be everywhere, neither corporation has that many stores.[2]

This book explores the history of one of those libraries, the Arlington Hills branch of the St. Paul Public Library on the city's East Side. It was one of three impressive branch libraries built in 1917 with a grant from Andrew Carnegie. Although focused on the Arlington Hills branch, the book also touches on the origins of its two siblings, the St. Anthony Park Public Library and the Riverview Public Library on the city's West Side. These neighborhood libraries were part of a major reinvention of the idea of the public library in the early 20th century. Gone were the days when the only library building was in the downtown business district. Cities began building libraries in working class neighborhoods where new immigrants were settling. In 2017, these three libraries celebrated their centennial, along with the George Latimer Central Library on Rice Park. By that time, however, the Carnegie-funded Arlington Hills library had already been reinvented for a second time, as the East Side Freedom Library.

Public libraries did not miraculously appear. We have them because a broad popular movement campaigned for them. Committed individuals worked in them, volunteered to serve on library boards, and organized "friends of the library" groups to support them. To defend them we need to understand their origins, their development, their strengths and their weaknesses, and to keep them central to our communities, we have to be willing to reinvent them.

Over the century of their existence, these libraries dealt with many changes. One of these changes is growth. Libraries everywhere tend to serve many more patrons than they did a century ago, circulate many more books, and provide a wider range of services. Another change is technological. Librarians in 1917, for example, could never have imagined that thousands of neighbors a century later would depend on the public library for internet access. Attitudes toward architecture have also changed. To judge by the grand stairways of Carnegie-era libraries, little thought was given to physical accessibility. Today we understand that if libraries are to retain their status as the most democratic of our public institutions, they must be accessible to all. Those libraries that have survived were altered with street-level entrances and elevators.

Grappling with these changes, towns and cities have sometimes decided to move out of a historic library and build anew. In the past, this often meant that a Carnegie library was demolished. In recent decades however, the desire to preserve historic buildings has deepened. As a result, libraries from this era are now much more likely to be remodeled for continued use. The St. Anthony Park and Riverview branches are still in operation, but in 2014, St. Paul built a new Arlington Hills Public Library as part of a community center on Payne Avenue.

This created the opportunity for a new kind of "free space" in the building that Carnegie contributed to the East Side. Historically, "free spaces" have been places where knowledge of how to nurture and expand the public good has been created and shared. Before the Europeans arrived in Minnesota, the Dakota had storytelling circles where elders passed down what they had learned, and this tradition continues today. Later, other kinds of free spaces were created, like the farmers' cooperatives that launched the Populist Party; the women's clubs and settlement houses that helped build a mass movement for suffrage in the early 20th century; the churches that provided the backbone of the anti-slavery and Civil Rights Movements; and the union halls which were the home base for workers' struggles. Our shared history teaches that "free spaces" are a crucial building block of democratic life. When times are tough, we need to protect existing "free spaces" and build new ones.[3]

Beth Cleary and Peter Rachleff, two long-time East Siders, formed a non-profit which negotiated a long-term lease for the former Arlington Hills Public Library and created the East Side Freedom Library. This represented another reinvention of the library idea, and a new kind of "free space" for the East Side. In addition to being a research library focused on immigrant, labor, and social justice history, the new library hosts a wide variety of programs including music, theater, films, lectures, roundtables, and community forums. It is also a gathering place where trade unionists, immigrant organizations, and neighbors can share concerns, ideas, and stories.

Over the years, the neighborhood around the library has been home to three waves of immigrants. Beginning in the 1850s, northern Europeans built the neighborhood and the labor movement in St. Paul. In the 1890s through World War I, they were joined by immigrants from southern and eastern Europe. Mexicans and African-Americans began to move to the East Side in the 1920s, and more recently, immigrants from Central America, East Africa and Southeast Asia found a home in the neighborhood. It is difficult for people to live and work together effectively if they don't know their own stories and the stories of others. The East Side Freedom Library provides a "free space" where these communities can research and share their stories. As the saying goes, "this is what democracy looks like."

- Introduction Endnotes -

[1] Eric Klinenberg, "Worry Less About Crumbling Roads, More About Crumbling Libraries," posted on *City Lab* and *The Atlantic* websites, September 21, 2018. See also his *Palaces for the People: How Social Infrastructure Can Help Fight Inequality, Polarization, and the Decline of Civic Life* (New York: Crown, 2018).

[2] "ALA Library Fact Sheet No 1." American Library Association website. https://libguides.ala.org/numberoflibraries (accessed January 29, 2019).

[3] Sara M. Evans and Harry G. Boyte, *Free Spaces: The Sources of Democratic Change in America* (New York: Harper & Row, 1986).

This book traces the history of the library, starting in Chapter One with the city of St. Paul's decision to create a tax-supported public library in the 19th Century. The city, however, was not willing to provide an adequate physical space for the library. By the time funding was found for the downtown library, it was clear that the city also needed branch libraries in the neighborhoods. Chapter Two tells the story of how Andrew Carnegie funded the city's first three branch libraries, including Arlington Hills, and why the buildings look the way they do. Since the Arlington Hills Public Library serves the needs of the East Side, Chapter Three describes the early history of the East Side and the library's connection to the community. Chapter Four notes the arrival of new immigrants from Asia and Latin America to the East Side, and also remembers some of the traumas the library and the community have weathered, including the departure of major industrial employers and a string of recessions that threatened the very existence of the Arlington Hills branch. The last chapter tells the story of how the city's decision to leave the historic library building in 2014 opened the path to its reinvention as the East Side Freedom Library, an institution which continues to thrive and grow.

- Chapter One -

A Free Public Library for St. Paul

From Downtown to the Neighborhoods

Midwestern towns and cities have public libraries today because a popular movement campaigned for them during the early years of European settlement. The Yankee settlers, who rushed to the valleys of the Mississippi, Minnesota, and St. Croix rivers to settle the lands taken from the Ojibwe and Dakota, brought with them an interest in books and learning. Even before statehood in 1858, eleven local groups sponsored some sort of library, the first of which was the St. Anthony Library Association in 1849.[1]

The first American libraries, however, were neither public nor free. Some were organized by entrepreneurs like Benjamin Franklin, who joined with other Philadelphians to organize a stock company to provide library services to shareholders. Others were organized by cultural organizations like the Boston Athenaeum which sponsored libraries for their members. Some libraries were organized by groups calling themselves Lyceums, which sponsored debates and lectures as well as libraries. These libraries were private affairs, even if they sometimes provided public reading rooms. They are called "subscription libraries" because only those who bought a share or paid an annual subscription could borrow books.

The St. Paul Library Association

St. Paul began to take shape on the banks of the Mississippi River in the late 1840s. A post office was established in 1846, and the village was platted the next year. By that time, there was regular steamboat service, and the city grew rapidly. There were barely 1,000 people in 1850, but that number had increased tenfold by 1860. European-American settlers came for the land, either to farm it or to cut timber, and for the economic opportunities that would follow with rapid population growth.[2]

By the mid-1850s, two organizations had started subscription libraries. The St. Paul branch of the Young Men's Christian Association (YMCA) organized a subscription library with a reading room opened to the public. About the same time, a group called the Mercantile Library Association opened a library that charged a $5 fee to join, plus a $3 annual fee. Subscription libraries tended to struggle financially, and true to form, the YMCA library closed in 1858 for lack of funds. However, a group of church women organized a successful fundraiser, and in 1861, reopened the YMCA library on the second-floor room of the Ingersoll Block on Bridge Square in downtown St. Paul. The Mercantile Library Association also struggled financially and was forced to close in 1861. When it reopened in 1863, St. Paul had two competing libraries, neither of which was sustainable financially.[3]

The boards of the two rival libraries solved this problem by agreeing to a merger that created the St. Paul Library Association. The new library, which now held twice as many books, continued to operate from the Ingersoll Block site. For a short time, Edward Eggleston, a young itinerant minister, served as librarian. He went on to become a nationally known writer of fiction for both adults and children, and later in life, a historian and president of the American Historical Association. The new library was funded by the sale of shares, including a lifetime share of $50, which included borrowing privileges, or by subscription fees of $2 per year. Only shareholders had a voice in governance. Some wealthy patrons bought many shares, but there were only about 300 subscribers.[4]

St. Paul's subscription library was similar to those in the other major urban areas in Minnesota. Duluth had a functioning subscription library with a full-time librarian for several years in the early 1870s. In Winona, the Young Men's Library Association opened a subscription library in 1863. When it became clear that women were the mainstays of the library, the name was changed to the Winona Library Association in 1873. Financial problems led to its closure in 1875, but a group of women resurrected it in 1877.

Minneapolis had the largest and most successful subscription library. A Young Men's Library Association was organized in 1859 and soon evolved into the Minneapolis Athenaeum. As a result of fundraising and a major bequest, it had over 4,000 volumes by 1875 and its own building. About two dozen other Minnesota towns also had subscription libraries in the 1860s and 1870s.[5]

These libraries could not survive on the sale of shares and subscriptions; they had to organize fundraisers to stay afloat. In the 1860s and 1870s, the most dependable fundraiser was an annual lecture series. In the days before radio and television, lectures by famous orators offered audiences an attractive combination of entertainment and enlightenment. The St. Paul Library Association hosted many nationally known speakers at the St. Paul Opera House, including Ralph Waldo Emerson, Horace Greeley, Elizabeth Cady Stanton, Susan B. Anthony, and Wendell Phillips. The biggest draw was Frederick Douglass, the most famous African-American in the country and a renowned public orator.

The Public Library Movement in Minnesota

In the early years of settlement, European-Americans tended to look "back East" for inspiration, especially in the realm of culture. What they saw back there was the growth of "free public libraries" supported by taxation, especially in the New England states from which many of them had migrated. The first tax-supported public library was in Petersborough, New Hampshire in 1833, followed in the 1840s by the Boston Public Library, the grandfather of big city public libraries (and still our largest library after the Library of Congress). However, a legal barrier stood in the way of public libraries. Towns and cities could not legally fund a library with tax money unless authorized by their state legislature. Library advocates had their first breakthrough in 1877 when Indiana and Iowa passed laws allowing public libraries. The Minnesota Legislature joined them in 1879.[6]

The way was now cleared for any Minnesota city or town to create a public library. City governments, however, were reluctant to take on the permanent support of a new institution, the benefits of which were not as obvious as, for example, the fire department.

A campaign for a public library was waged in every locality, usually led by the leaders of the local subscription library. In the decade following the passage of the Minnesota law, thirteen city councils were persuaded to take the plunge, including St. Paul in 1882, Minneapolis in 1885, and Winona in 1886. Twenty-two more cities, including Duluth, created public libraries by 1900, and eventually, all subscription libraries were replaced by tax-supported libraries.[7]

The leaders of the St. Paul Library Association led the campaign in St. Paul. The president of the association was Alexander Ramsey, who had earlier led a campaign to drive Native Americans out of the Minnesota territory and make their lands available to white settlers and developers. Later he served terms as St. Paul mayor, the first territorial governor, the second governor of the state, a United States Senator, and the Secretary of War. As soon as the legislature cleared the way for public libraries, he told the St. Paul City Council that if the city created a tax-supported public library, the association would donate its books and furnishings. The council turned him down. Three years later, with the city's financial situation improved, Ramsey tried again. This time the council voted 8 to 2 to create the St. Paul Public Library and appropriate $5,000 for its development. The association turned over its book collection, which had grown to 8,000, and its second-floor space in the Ingersoll Block.[8]

The council created a nine-member library board, and the mayor then appointed Alexander Ramsey as president, Maurice Auerbach as vice-president, and William H. Kelley as secretary—who were, respectively, a neat combination of a Pennsylvania-born son of a Scottish immigrant, a successful financier born in Germany, and an Irish-American. The board chose Helen J. McCaine to be the library director, and she officially opened the St. Paul Public Library on the day after New Year's Day, 1883. She had served as the head librarian of the St. Paul Library Association since 1877 and went on to lead the public library until her retirement in 1913, a tenure as the city's chief librarian which lasted 37 years.[9] Remarkably, she had been born in Petersborough, New Hampshire, the first town in the country to organize a public library.[10]

As happened in many places, the public library in St. Paul was immediately popular. The St. Paul Library Association had never attracted more than 400 subscribers. By the end of 1884, the St. Paul

Public Library had almost 3,500 subscribers registered for a library card. By 1889, the number had reached 6,200, and the number of residents using the public library would continue to grow. The book collection also grew from 8,000 at the beginning to over 21,000 by 1889.[11] Although the library expanded into the third floor of the Ingersoll Block, more space was needed. St. Paulites could not help but notice that across the river, the Minneapolis Public Library was about to move into a new building, financed by city bonds supplemented by the gifts of businessmen like lumberman T. B. Walker.

The Search for a Permanent Home

The Chamber of Commerce and the local newspapers supported the idea of a new building for the St. Paul Public Library. The city leaders, however, tended to think that their responsibility to the library ended when they authorized a tax for its operating expenses. Meanwhile, they were in the process of building a large stone building on Fourth Street which would house the city hall as well as the county courthouse. It was a smaller version of the Minneapolis City Hall which was built about the same time, and whereas the Minneapolis building is still in use today, the St. Paul version was demolished in 1933.[12] The city refused to build a library, but was willing to give the library some space in the new city hall. In 1889, the St. Paul Public Library settled into the new building and stayed for a decade, although the library board never felt that this space

St. Paul City Hall and Ramsey County Courthouse, at Fourth and Wabasha, was the home of the St. Paul Public Library from 1889 to 1899.

would be adequate to their needs.

James J. Hill

In fact, the library's quest for a permanent home was only just beginning. Having gotten nowhere with the city council, the library board turned to private philanthropy. This inevitably led library advocates to the door of the city's richest man, the railroad magnate James J. Hill, who was just then planning his great mansion on Summit Hill overlooking the city. The library board approached him in 1890, but apparently, the city could not or would not agree to the conditions he set on a major gift. Shortly thereafter, he gave $500,000 to the Catholic Church to build the St. Paul Seminary.[13]

The idea was then floated to fund a new library by selling Market Hall, which the city had built in 1881 as a public market and meeting hall.[14] The public market had quickly outgrown the building which had become a burden to the city. This plan might have worked, but before anything had been done, the depression called the "Panic of 1893" intervened and deflated the property values in the city. The proceeds of a sale would no longer be enough to build a new library. This led to another temporary fix. In 1899, the city gave Market Hall to the library, with the understanding that the first floor would be rented to shops and the library would use the second floor. The rental income would pay for the remodeling of the library's space. In the summer of 1899, the library moved from city hall to Market Hall.[15]

Business leaders then shifted their strategy. Since James J. Hill continued to stonewall them, they sent letters to Andrew Carnegie asking him to finance a library building in downtown St. Paul. This made sense. Carnegie had funded libraries in his home town of Pittsburgh and several other Pennsylvania towns associated with his steel plants during the 1880s, and he had just then begun his "wholesale" gifts of libraries to towns and cities. Eventually, he would fund the building of about 2,500 library buildings around the English-speaking world.[16]

Edward Chittenden, an attorney active in the Commercial Club, made the plea to James Bertram, the man who managed Andrew Carnegie's library program. To bolster his case, Chittenden arranged for architect Cass Gilbert to prepare sketches of a new library and send them to Carnegie. Bertram responded that Carnegie "felt it would be indelicate for him to become the donor" of a library in St. Paul because Judge Henry Hale had left a bequest to the library. In fact, the estate was in property which had lost much of his value, and there were restrictions on how and when it could be used. Chittenden wrote Bertram explaining that the Hale estate could not help the city, and he even had Judge Hale's widow write to Carnegie to clarify the situation.[17] Carnegie would not budge. Chittenden tried again in 1903, this time backed up by a letter signed by the mayor, the Chamber of Commerce president, the Commercial Club president, the judges of the district court, the superintendent of schools, and even John Ireland, the Catholic archbishop of St. Paul. Carnegie was unmoved.[18] Very likely, Carnegie was reluctant not because of the Hale Estate but because he felt that James J. Hill was duty-bound to build the public library in his home town, just as Carnegie had done in Pittsburgh.[19]

There things sat, until 1910, when Mayor David Lawler proposed selling Market Hall for whatever it was worth. Meanwhile, the library board decided that the property on the south side of Rice Park would be the best place for the library. While the council and the library board wrangled about how to proceed, David Chauncey Shepard, a wealthy railroad contractor, offered $100,000 towards the project if other donors would come forward. This apparently provoked James J. Hill to offer $250,000, and in 1912, he raised his offer to $750,000 if the city would supply the site and if the new library building would house both the public library and the privately-controlled reference library he had long dreamed of building. The city issued the bonds, and a group of private donors pitched in another $100,000 towards the land purchase.[20]

At Hill's suggestion, the city hired New York architect Electus Litchfield to design the building. He created the elegant Renaissance Revival building which stands on the river side of Rice Park. The Fourth Street façade of the marble-clad building features two arched entrances reached by stairways, reflecting the fact that the building is the home of two separate institutions, the St. Paul Public Library and the Hill Reference Library.[21] As was the case with most libraries from this era, those impressive marble stairways would eventually be recognized as accessibility barriers to be overcome.

Although construction began in 1914, the public library wing was not formally dedicated until 1917, and the reference library not until 1921. While the St. Paul Public Library was waiting to make its final move to a permanent home, disaster struck. On April 27, 1915, a gas explosion started a fire that destroyed Market Hall and the books, periodicals and furniture of the St. Paul Public Library. By that time, the library's book collection had grown to over 158,000 books. Fortunately, about 34,000 were circulating out of the building when the fire struck. Three days later, the St. Paul Public Library opened in House of Hope Church at Fifth and Exchange, yet another temporary home. The community rallied around the library and donations of books quickly led to a collection larger than what the library had before the fire. In May 1916, the library moved into a section of the

Firefighters extinguish the 1915 fire at Market Hall, which had been the St. Paul Public Library's home since 1899. The library's book and periodical collection was largely destroyed.

unfinished new building on Rice Park. There were no more surprises, and the headquarters of the St. Paul Public Library never moved again.[22]

The Outreach of Women

The boards which governed the newly created public libraries were generally composed of wealthy entrepreneurs and well-to-do professionals, most of whom were men. Meanwhile, women dominated the growing profession of librarian, taking the lead in operating, maintaining, and transforming libraries nationwide. Women filled most positions in libraries big and small, and like Helen McCaine in St. Paul, often held the position of chief librarian. In Minnesota, as historian Paul Ostendorf observed, "the creation of libraries...was definitely the work of women."[23] However, the patriarchal nature of American society guaranteed that a profession dominated by women would suffer economically.

Two remarkable women stand out as leaders of the public library movement in Minnesota. Born in Hastings, Gratia Countryman joined the staff of the Minneapolis Public Library in 1889 after graduating from the University of Minnesota, and by 1904 had risen to the position of head librarian. She was legendary for her efforts to bring library services to underserved communities.[24] Clara Baldwin, a Lake City native and part of Countryman's circle at the university, was hired in 1899 by the newly created State Public Library Commission to create a system of traveling libraries. Eventually, Baldwin became head of the commission, and when it was replaced by the Library

Gratia Countryman

Division of the Department of Education in 1919, she led the new agency, a position she held until her retirement in 1936. She developed an extensive system of "traveling libraries" throughout the state, and used them as a springboard for building permanent public libraries in every county.[25] Countryman and Baldwin, in other words, were the inspirational leaders of the many women who were working to reinvent the public library as an institution that would reach people of all classes in all corners of the state.[26] Nevertheless, when Countryman became head of the Minneapolis library in 1904, she was offered a $2,000 salary, which was $1,000 less than what her predecessor James Hosmer had earned.[27]

Clara Baldwin

Across the river, McCaine led the St. Paul Public Library through a period of remarkable growth. She had a reputation as a traditional librarian interested, above all, in building the book collection, and in fact she was responsible for the large collection that was destined to be largely destroyed by the 1915 fire. While she was chief librarian, the number of users with library cards reached a total of 37,672. In 1914, the cardholders checked out books 584,500 times.[28] Countryman and Baldwin were encouraging librarians to make their libraries welcoming places for children. St. Paul had, in fact, opened a children's room in 1894, and by 1914, children's literature accounted for 18 percent of the total circulation.[29]

McCaine may not have been as innovative as her counterpart in Minneapolis, but she had the good sense to follow Gratia Countryman's lead in reinventing the library by extending its services into the neighborhoods. The city was growing rapidly, and new residential communities were developing in all directions. The downtown library was increasingly distant from where most people

Helen McCaine

lived. In response, McCaine began a school library service in 1907. At first, a mini-library of 50 books was sent to the ten largest schools. By 1914, the program was circulating almost 143,000 books to 43 schools. This represented 24 percent of the total circulation of the library. This brought children's books into the neighborhoods, but did nothing to meet the needs of adults.

Prior to 1900, some big city libraries began bringing books to the neighborhoods by means of "delivery stations," small spaces in retail establishments where patrons could order books which would be delivered from the downtown library. The next step was a "branch," which at first was just a small rented storefront with a part-time staff. The building of permanent branch libraries was accelerated by Andrew Carnegie, who helped build branch libraries in Pittsburgh in the 1880s, and then gave New York City a huge grant to build 66 branches throughout the boroughs in 1899. Grants to build branches in other large cities soon followed.[30]

By that time, librarians recognized that there was a powerful unmet hunger for books and periodicals in the growing working-class neighborhoods of every city. Thanks to the common school movement, literacy rates among workers approached 100 percent by the turn of the century. The enormous growth of newspapers in those years was fueled by a working-class public which was hungry for all the newspapers had to offer, including serialized fiction. In the days before radio, the reading of fiction, whether in a newspaper or in "dime novels," was a major part of working-class entertainment.[31]

Reflecting this demand, the early trade unions played a role in the public library movement. In 1835, the National Trades' Union, the first national labor federation in the United States, urged all its affiliates to agitate for free public libraries.[32] Unions also created their own resources for their members. By the early years of the twentieth century, union halls in the Twin Cities often featured "reading rooms" where newspapers, magazines, and a few books were available. For example, the Building Trades Council in Minneapolis opened a reading room at its headquarters in 1907. It was heavily patronized, and led to similar reading rooms in the halls of separate unions.[33] Many trade union newspapers, including the *Minnesota Union Advocate* published by the St. Paul Trades and Labor Assembly, regularly featured fiction. In 1914, for example, the labor newspaper featured as many as four short stories in a given issue.[34]

The delivery stations were a stop-gap measure to meet this demand for reading material. Gratia Countryman's Minneapolis library had ten delivery stations and three small branches by 1904. McCaine opened five transfer stations in 1905 and had eleven by 1912, spread out through St. Paul's growing neighborhoods. The library would deliver about 200 books to each station and exchange them every three months. In addition, a messenger visited each station weekly to fill patron orders. The most common location was a drug store. Since the library owned no property and paid no rent, the library could afford to maintain a wide network of stations. The retailers were paid 1 cent for each book circulated over 1,000 in a year. The messengers were paid 25 cents per station plus carfare. Traffic at these stations demonstrated the growing hunger for library services in the neighborhoods. In 1905, only about 5 percent of the library's total circulation was through the stations. By 1914, almost 125,000 books were loaned by the library through the stations, representing 21 percent of the total circulation.[35]

The story of the Arlington Hills Public Library begins with the delivery station which the library established on the East Side, one of the five stations with which the library began the program in 1905. Called "Station B," it was located in Bodin's Drug Store on Payne Avenue. This business was a partnership begun in 1895 by John Bodin and Victor Sundberg. In about 1900, they moved their store into a new building at 881 Payne, the original location of Station B. East Siders borrowed 7,000 books from the station in its first year of operation, and three years later, over 12,000 books were loaned from

Library day at a school transfer station.

Station B. Bodin's Drug Store later moved again, this time to 896 Payne, where the store continued to host Station B until the Arlington Hills branch of the St. Paul Public Library opened in 1917.[36] As we will see, Victor Sundberg played a major role in bringing a branch library to the East Side.

Helen McCaine was 78 in 1913 and decided to let a younger person manage the transition to the new downtown library which was then in the planning stages. At its January 2, 1914 meeting, the library board passed a resolution accepting her resignation and thanking her for her work. At that same meeting, the board hired William Dawson Johnston, the head librarian at Columbia University in New York, as the new librarian, effective immediately.[37] A history of St. Paul published prior to her resignation noted that no one was "entitled to more credit" for the growth and effectiveness of the library than McCaine, who was called "the ever-faithful and ever-capable librarian."[38] Nevertheless, after 37 years as head librarian, her annual salary in 1913 was only $1,500, roughly equivalent to about $37,000 today. The board set William Dawson Johnston's starting salary at $4,500 for 1914, a remarkable testament to the wage discrimination of the age. Although the salaries of a few of the librarians who served under McCaine were $1,200, most were between $700 and 900, so that their average salary was equivalent to about $20,000 today.[39] The women who built the public libraries were like the women who taught for very little pay in the thousands of common schools throughout Minnesota. The spread of public schooling and the growth of public libraries were both fueled by the seriously undervalued labor of women.

In any case, McCaine retired just in time to avoid some new difficulties. Johnston was hired just as a new city charter ended the library board. The head of the library now served under the Commissioner of Education, who was a city council member appointed to oversee the Department of Education which included the library.[40] He also had to deal with the loss of most of the library's books and periodicals in the Market Hall fire while managing the transition to the new library on Rice Park. Johnston was an energetic spokesperson for the library and put much energy into publicizing it. He enthusiastically followed the path of Countryman and Baldwin in expanding library services beyond downtown.

By 1914, it was clear that St. Paul needed to go beyond transfer stations and build permanent branch libraries in the neighborhoods. Johnston and the library board had made branch libraries a priority. From where would the money come? Across the river, Minneapolis had secured a grant from Andrew Carnegie to build four branch libraries. Now that James J. Hill had committed himself to funding the downtown library, maybe Carnegie would, at last, be open to helping St. Paul.

A Closer Look...

Frederick Douglass in 1866, the year before his first lecture tour to Minnesota.

Frederick Douglass in Minnesota

After the Civil War, Frederick Douglass traveled the lecture circuit throughout the northern states. Audiences were fascinated by this formerly enslaved man who had become a leader of the abolition movement and a confidant of Abraham Lincoln. An imposing, broad-shouldered man with a commanding presence, he had mastered the technique of giving lectures laced with wit and humor that both entertained and instructed. His early topics included slavery and the anti-slavery movement, the Civil War, Reconstruction, and most important to him, voting rights for former enslaved people. Later he added lectures on a wide variety of historical and social issues.[41]

Douglass traveled to Minnesota four times on lecture tours. In 1867, local library associations sponsored his lectures in Winona, St. Paul, and Minneapolis. His only Minnesota stop in 1868 was in Rochester. The library associations of Minneapolis and St. Paul brought him back in 1869, and during that trip, he also lectured in Mankato. He returned to St. Paul in 1873 for a lecture sponsored by the Grand Army of the Republic, an organization of Civil War veterans. This trip also included stops in Minneapolis and Anoka. He returned to Minnesota many years later for the 1892 Republican National Convention, and while in Minneapolis, he spoke at a women's suffrage rally with Susan B. Anthony and at an African-American church.

His lectures were major events. The *St. Paul Dispatch* promised its readers that his 1869 lecture would be "the greatest treat of the lecture season." Following the event, the newspaper highly rated the two-hour lecture, and noted that the library association must have been gladdened by the full house. When Douglass returned in 1873, the *Minneapolis Tribune* wrote that his lecture "will undoubtedly prove to be an intellectual treat and this fact should serve to fill every seat." It dared its racist readers to attend, since if they thought he was below them, "possibly they might conclude that 'the boot is on the other leg.'"

Douglass often met with discrimination, and unfortunately, he was denied lodging at two St. Paul hotels in 1873, provoking a flurry of newspaper editorials denouncing the hotel owners. The *St. Paul Dispatch,* however, argued that it was all a "tempest in a teapot," and that one of the hotels had offered Douglass a free meal by way of apology and Douglass, in fact, had stayed there. Another newspaper responded that the apology only came after a group of state legislators staying in the hotel threatened to move to a Minneapolis establishment in protest.[42]

Ironically, the lecture he was scheduled to give that night was entitled "Composite Nation," a stirring call for the United States to embrace its destiny as a multicultural society. In particular, Douglass defended Asian immigrants against the racist backlash of those years. "I want a home here not only for the Negro, the mulatto, and the Latin races," he told his audiences, "but I want the Asiatic to find a home in the United States and feel at home here, both for his sake and ours." The only wise policy, he argued, was "a liberal and brotherly welcome to all who are likely to come to the United States."[43]

As is often the case, Douglass' words seem fresh and timely, and an inspiration for libraries of all kinds.

- Chapter 1 Endnotes -

[1] Ellsworth Carlstedt, "The Public Library Movement in Minnesota 1849–1900," *Minnesota Libraries,* September 1945, p. 351.

[2] Theodore C. Blegen, *Minnesota: A History of the State,* 2nd Edition (Minneapolis: University of Minnesota Press, 1963, 1975), p. 156–159, 177.

[3] Henry A. Castle, *History of St. Paul and Vicinity* (Chicago: Lewis Pub. Co, 1912), p. 478–479; Gary Phelps, "The St. Paul Library and its First 100 Years," *Ramsey County History* 18, No. 1 (1982): 3–4; Bilone W. Young, *A Noble Task: The St. Paul Public Library Celebrates 125!* (Afton, MN: Afton Historical Press, 2007), p. 23–28.

[4] Young, p. 28–29, 38; John T. Flanagan, "The Hoosier Schoolmaster in Minnesota," *Minnesota History* 18, No 4 (1937): 347–370.

[5] Carlstedt, p. 351–356; Greg Gaut, *Laird's Legacy: A History of the Winona Public Library* (Winona: Friends of the Winona Public Library, 2016), p. 11–13.

[6] Carlstedt, p. 358.

[7] Carlstedt, p. 359.

[8] Young, p. 42.

[9] Young, p. 47.

[10] Castle, p. 1167

[11] Phelps, p. 7.

[12] Larry Millett, *Lost Twin Cities* (St. Paul: Minnesota Historical Society Press, 1992), p. 206–207.

[13] Young, p. 53–54.

[14] Millett, p. 150–151.

[15] Young, p. 55–56.

[16] George S. Bobinski, *Carnegie Libraries: Their History and Impact on American Public Library Development* (Chicago: American Library Association, 1969); Abigail A. Van Slyck, *Free to All: Carnegie Libraries and American Culture 1890–1920* (Chicago: University of Chicago Press, 1995); Theodore Jones, *Carnegie Libraries across America: A Public Legacy* (New York: John Wiley, 1997); Durand R. Miller, *Carnegie Grants for Library Buildings 1890–1917* (New York: Carnegie Corporation, 1943).

[17] James Bertram to Edward S. Chittenden, June 22, 1901; Edward Chittenden to James Bertram, July 15, 1901; Mary E. Hale to Andrew Carnegie, July 10, 1901. Carnegie Corporation of New York Records, Columbia University Libraries, Series II Files on Microfilm, Part A.1 Libraries, Reel 27. Correspondence in the Carnegie files is organized by community. All letters to or from St. Paul are in Reel 27.

[18] Mayor of the City of St. Paul and others to Andrew Carnegie, January 15, 1903; James Bertram to Edward S. Chittenden, February 20, 1903.

[19] Phelps, p. 10.

[20] Young, p. 60–61.

[21] Young, p. 63–67.

[22] Phelps, p. 14.

[23] Paul Ostendorf, *The History of the Public Library Movement in Minnesota from 1849 to 1916* (Ph.D dissertation, University of Minnesota, 1984), p. 68.

[24] Jane Pejsa, *Gratia Countryman: Her Life, Her Loves, and Her Library* (Minneapolis: Nodin Press, 1995).

[25] Robert F. Garland, "The Other Librarian: Clara Baldwin and the Public Library Movement in Minnesota," 42 *Ramsey County History,* No 3 (Fall 1907): 4–10.

[26] See also Ostendorf for detailed accounts of the importance of Countryman (p 378–397) and Baldwin (p 397–403).

[27] This provoked considerable protest among librarians and those fighting for women's suffrage. Bruce Weir Benidt, *The Library Book: A Centennial History of the Minneapolis Public Library* (Minneapolis: Minneapolis Public Library, 1984), 75–76. Baldwin, by the way, was paid $1,200 in 1903 to lead the State Library Commission. Garland, p. 7.

[28] Annual Report of the Public Library for the City of St. Paul for the year ending December 31, 1914.

[29] Phelps, p. 11.

[30] Van Slyck, p. 101.

[31] Michael Denning, *Mechanical Accents: Dime Novels and Working Class Culture in America* (New York: Verso, 1987), p. 46.

[32] Philip S. Foner, *History of the Labor Movement in the United States,* Vol 1 (New York: International Publishers, 1947), p. 115.

[33] "Union Reading Rooms," *Minneapolis Labor Review,* November 21, 1907, p. 5.

[34] See for example the January 14, 1914 issue of *Minnesota Union Advocate* which features four separate pieces of short fiction.

[35] Annual Report, 1914.

[36] East Side Commercial Club, *A Souvenir of the Payne Avenue Carnival and Street Fair, 1906* [printed booklet] in the archives of the Minnesota Historical Society; Annual Report, 1917.

[37] Minutes of the St. Paul Public Library Board of Directors, Vol 3, January 2, 1914.

[38] Castle, p. 1197.

[39] Minutes of the St. Paul Public Library Board of Directors, Vol 3, January 27, 1914.

[40] Annual Report 1914.

[41] David W. Blight, *Frederick Douglass: Prophet of Freedom* (New York: Simon & Schuster, 2018), p. 470, 527–528.

[42] This event is analyzed in detail in William D. Green's *Degrees of Freedom: The Origins of Civil Rights in Minnesota* (Minneapolis: University of Minnesota Press, 2015), p. 103–114.

[43] Philip Foner and Robert Branhan, *Lift Every Voice: African-American Oratory 1787–1900* (Tuscaloosa: University of Alabama Press, 1998), p. 488–503.

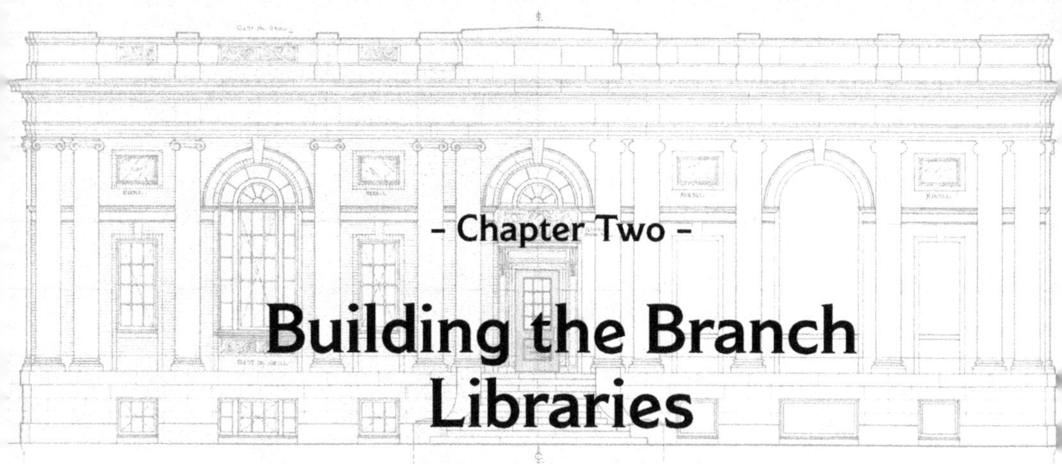

- Chapter Two -

Building the Branch Libraries

The Support of Andrew Carnegie

Since Andrew Carnegie stonewalled them earlier, the library board approached him carefully in 1914 with a request to fund branch libraries in the neighborhoods. Board member Charles Ames, president of West Publishing, wrote to a personal friend at the Carnegie Corporation and tactfully expressed sympathy with Andrew Carnegie's suggestion that "local citizens," that is, James J. Hill, should pay for the downtown library. Things worked out well, Ames noted, and Hill agreed to fund the library on Rice Park. The board moved on to the "crying need for eight or nine branch libraries." Ames thought the city could raise money for three of them. Could Carnegie help with the rest? [1]

The reply came from James Bertram, Carnegie's personal secretary, who wanted to know about the locations of the proposed branches, the possibility of other funding, and the city's commitment to support its growing library system.[2] Ames responded that there were perhaps ten districts in St. Paul that would eventually need branch libraries, but that no neighborhood had been selected. The city hoped to build some branches with Judge Hale's bequest when it finally became available.[3] Bertram responded that St. Paul might apply for funding for half the number of branches it had in mind, but only if the city had a definite plan for their long-term support.[4]

The city moved quickly. On May 1, 1914, the president of the Library Board and the mayor submitted a formal request to Bertram for $75,000 to fund three branch libraries.[5] Although there had been no public discussions about which neighborhoods would get the first branch libraries, the letter was quite specific:

"A" First Ward, Arlington Hills: largely Scandinavian; population 1910: 24,000; about 5,000 school children in the district.
Request for this branch... $30,000

"B" Sixth Ward, West Side: largely Hebrew; population 1910: 22,000; 4,800 school children and they have no opportunity at home to read since their houses are crowded.
Request for this branch... $20,000

"C" St. Anthony Park, North: five-and-a-half miles from the center of the city; largely residential; population 1910: 11,000; about 1,500 school children; better class of residences.
Request for this branch... $25,000

Anticipating Carnegie's requirements, the city promised to find suitable sites and to fund the maintenance of the libraries at 10 percent of the grant amount annually. The letter did not explain how these three neighborhoods were chosen or why different amounts were requested for each library. Bertram quickly wrote back granting the request, adding the normal condition that plans would have to be submitted for his approval prior to construction.[6] The city then announced the grant to the press.[7]

The Carnegie Library Program

By 1914, Andrew Carnegie had been funding libraries in towns and cities for more than thirty years. His generosity was made possible by the great wealth he had accumulated by forcing immigrant iron miners, coal miners, and steel workers to work long hours for poor pay. When workers resisted, he did everything he could to break their unions. In 1892, his subordinate, Henry Clay Frick, imposed a 12-hour day on the workers at his Homestead, Pennsylvania steel plant and then sent in an army of Pinkerton agents to break their strike. In the battle that followed, more than a dozen died.[8]

In 1901, he sold all his companies to J. P. Morgan and became, as Morgan observed, "the richest man in the world." He had been an active philanthropist before that, but now he retired from business and made philanthropy his major pursuit. Carnegie's gifts to public libraries were probably the best-known aspect of his wide-

Andrew Carnegie

ranging philanthropy. In the United States alone, he would donate approximately $42 million for the construction of 1,681 libraries between 1881 and 1919. He donated funds for over 800 more libraries in Scotland, England, Ireland, New Zealand, Australia, and elsewhere in the English-speaking world.

In the early years of his philanthropy, however, Carnegie only funded libraries in the Pennsylvania towns where he had steel plants and in Pittsburgh, which he considered his home town even though he no longer lived there. The only exception was a gift made to Fairfield, Iowa, the serendipitous result of a personal appeal by a United States Senator from Iowa. When built in 1893, it was the only "Carnegie library" outside of Pennsylvania, and the prototype for what Carnegie called the "wholesale" funding of libraries which began in 1898.[9]

Carnegie's first library gift in Minnesota was a $75,000 grant in 1899 for the downtown library in Duluth, an impressive Classical Revival building with an imposing dome. It was completed in 1902, and in that same year, libraries funded by Carnegie opened in Mankato, Stillwater, and St. Cloud. Eventually, Carnegie contributed nearly $1 million to the building of 65 public libraries in Minnesota, and in addition, he made a $30,000 grant to Hamline University in 1907 to build a library on its campus in St. Paul.[10]

Carnegie was perhaps the world's most famous businessman and philanthropist, but he also aspired to be a public intellectual. He published quite a few books and articles, but nothing matched the influence of the two famous essays published in the *North American Review* in 1889—now collectively referred to as "the Gospel of Wealth." In the first essay, Carnegie argued that the "duty of a man of wealth" was to live modestly, provide moderately for his dependents, and beyond that, "consider all surplus revenues which come to him simply as trust funds, which he is called upon to administer… to produce the most beneficial results for the community."[11] To him, living "modestly" meant owning several homes, including Skibo, the castle he expanded into a 200-room mansion in his native Scotland, and his 80-foot yacht, *Seabreeze*. In any case, Carnegie believed that he had solved the moral problem of inequality. However, his solution depended on the rich voluntarily following his advice. If they did not, he thought the "public verdict" should be this: "The man who dies thus rich, dies disgraced."[12]

In the second essay, he outlined the best way to contribute to the public good. The rich should give generously, he argued, to universities, libraries, hospitals, parks, meeting and concert halls, public baths, and church buildings. In his own case, he gave first place to the library, which was "the best gift which can be given to a community."[13] In his autobiography, Carnegie wrote that personal experiences led him to value libraries above all other gifts. He grew up in a family which valued books and reading. His father, a master weaver, organized a small library for the families of his fellow weavers. Most of the adult males in his extended family were members of the Chartist movement which was fighting to extend the vote to male workers. In 1848, the family emigrated to Allegheny, Pennsylvania, and the young Andrew Carnegie, then thirteen years old, took advantage of the personal library of a local man who opened his doors to working boys once a week.[14] Carnegie was, from adolescence, an advocate for free public libraries, which he famously characterized as "this republic of letters, where neither rank, office, nor wealth receives the slightest consideration."

As his philanthropic program expanded, Carnegie hired James Bertram, a young man from Scotland, as his personal secretary. Bertram took over the job of responding to the towns, cities, organizations, and individuals who sought support for various projects and causes. As news of Carnegie's giving spread, hundreds of cities and towns around the country sent letters to Carnegie inquiring about the possibility of a library. Over the years, Bertram refined the procedure for handling requests. Each applicant, including the St. Paul's library board, had to supply information about their city and their plans for building and maintaining a library. Bertram reviewed each applicant based on a simple set of criteria. He required that the city have a genuine public library supported by tax money in place. The city also had to have a suitable site secured, and the governing body had to agree to maintain the library in perpetuity at 10 percent of the total cost of the building's construction. Many places balked at this, but Carnegie refused to fund a library for a town which would not make a long-term commitment to sustain it.[15]

Bertram computed the size of the grant based on the population of the city as determined by the United States census, with a rough standard of $2 to $3 per capita.[16] There was no possibility of getting more. Carnegie, for example, offered Northfield, Minnesota, a library grant of $10,000 based on its population. Pointing to their two prestigious colleges, city officials asked that it be increased to $15,000 because they were an "exceptionally enterprising town" with "an unusually intelligent population." They needed a "handsomer and more suitable building" than $10,000 could buy. Bertram told Northfield that the amount offered was "quite up to standard of what he is doing for other towns of the same size."[17]

Branch libraries in cities were handled differently. Carnegie's enthusiasm for branch libraries was demonstrated in 1899 when he gave New York a $5 million grant to build 65 branch libraries. On the other hand, he wanted to make sure that towns and cities were willing and able to adequately maintain their growing library systems. Cities were warned not to bite off more than they could chew. As Bertram suggested to Ames, if St. Paul wanted funds for about six libraries, maybe they should ask for half of that. In Minnesota, the three largest cities asked for and received funding for branch libraries. Prior to St. Paul's successful application for three branch libraries, Carnegie had given $125,000 to build four branch libraries in Minneapolis, and grants totaling $50,000 for two branch libraries in Duluth.[18]

As he gained more experience, Bertram devised specific guidelines to govern his review of architectural drawings. To aid applicants, he produced a short pamphlet in 1911 entitled "Notes on the Erection of Public Libraries." Its basic principle was that the libraries should be functional buildings with no wasted space. Bertram recommended one-story rectangular buildings with a basement about four feet below street level. The basement should have 9- to 10-foot-high ceilings, which would leave the main floor about 5 to 6 feet above the street. He proposed 12- to 15-foot-high ceilings on the main floor and windows that start six feet above the floor to allow for wall space for bookshelves. He also included sketches of floor plans, "offered as suggestions." Except in the very smallest libraries, he recommended that the main floors be divided into adult and children's reading rooms. The basements, even in the smallest libraries, should contain a lecture hall, toilets, work and storage space, and a boiler room.[19] In correspondence with applicants, Bertram added that "smoking rooms" had no place in libraries, and that fireplaces took up wall space that should be used for bookshelves.[20]

Bertram's recommendations, backed up by the power of Carnegie's grants, had a major impact on library design. The suggested floor plans popularized "open stacks," the system by which books are shelved around the perimeter of the reading room rather than in a "stack room" which only librarians could enter. Now, everyone could browse the stacks for books. His plans also institutionalized the idea that children were welcome in libraries and deserved their own special area. The plans included a meeting hall, usually in the basement, which turned every library into a community center. This reformation of library design, coupled with the promotion of branch libraries in neighborhoods, amounted to a reinvention of the idea of the public library.

With respect to exteriors, Bertram's major concern was controlling costs. Cities were warned that they were not to build "Greek temples."[21] For example, almost all the Carnegie libraries in Minnesota are brick buildings with stone trim. A limestone, granite or marble exterior was not likely to be approved. Few Carnegie libraries have domes, which Bertram discouraged. However, Bertram said nothing in the "Notes" about architectural style. This was an area, he wrote, where "the community and the architect may express their individuality," so long as the result was a "simple, dignified structure."[22]

The Neighborhoods Rally

Carnegie offered to fund three branch libraries in St. Paul, but it was up to the city council to formally accept his conditions. At first, council members were cool to the idea, with various members expressing concerns about the increased tax burden. The *St. Paul Dispatch* editorialized that the city should build its own branch libraries "without any strings whatever." Some councilmembers apparently shared the newspaper's concern that "the original donation amounts to levying a burden in perpetuity upon the receiver of the gift." They harbored the suspicion that Carnegie was pushing them to expand the public library system faster than they might on their own, which, of course, was exactly what Carnegie was trying to do.[23]

There might also have been some of the resentment that many trade unionists felt towards Carnegie, whose enormous wealth was the result of a sordid record of union-busting. In particular, trade unionists could not forgive Carnegie for what had happened at Homestead in 1892. In Detroit, for example, local opposition to a $750,000 Carnegie grant, much of it from trade unions who felt that Carnegie's money was "tainted," delayed acceptance of the gift for

FORTY-MILLIONAIRE CARNEGIE IN HIS GREAT DOUBLE ROLE.
AS THE TIGHTFISTED EMPLOYER HE REDUCES WAGES THAT HE MAY PLAY PHILANTHROPIST AND GIVE AWAY LIBRARIES, ETC.

This 1892 political cartoon from *The Saturday Globe* in Utica, New York captures Carnegie's contradictions. He is shown as both a ruthless employer and a generous philanthropist.

eight years.[24] In Minneapolis, an effigy of Carnegie was turned into a "mangled corpse" at a 1912 Trades and Labor Assembly meeting where a resolution calling on the city to reject Carnegie's "blood money" was passed. The unions made it clear that they did not want a Carnegie library in the city because Carnegie "hired thugs and Pinkerton detectives to shoot down the strikers at Homestead years ago."[25]

On the other hand, the labor movement was a strong supporter of the public library movement and specifically advocated building branch libraries in the neighborhoods. The St. Paul Trades and Labor Assembly made a strong case for why the working people of St. Paul's neighborhoods needed branch libraries. Its newspaper, the *Minnesota Union Advocate,* argued that many working people have been "industrious users of the public library" for many years, but that now they "live at a considerable distance from the main building, and they frequently find it too much of a tax on their time and strength, after a hard day's work... to make the long trip to that building and back to their homes in the evening, however desirous they may be of using the library's means for their improvement." The newspaper concluded that "the branch libraries are badly needed for their development." This editorial, written in 1916 while the Carnegie libraries were under construction, made no mention of Carnegie, arguing instead that the trustees of the Judge Hale estate should make branch libraries a priority. [26]

The political situation was complicated by a new city charter which did away with independent bodies like the library board in favor of a system in which the city council chose each of its members to be the "commissioner" of a particular area of city services. The council chose Anthony Yoerg to be the "Commissioner of Education," essentially the head of a department which included the schools and the library. Community groups successfully lobbied Yoerg to put the library issue on the council agenda.[27] At a public hearing in July 1914, neighborhood representatives urged the council to accept Carnegie's money and staked their claim for one of the new buildings. Although the city's request had specifically mentioned Arlington Hills, the West Side, and St. Anthony Park, speakers also made a case for the Hamline and Dayton's Bluff neighborhoods.[28]

The recently appointed librarian, William Dawson Johnston, told the council that branch libraries were needed because the growth of the city meant that most children now lived at a great distance from the downtown library. He also reminded them about the new branch libraries being built in Minneapolis. Former library board chair E. A. Young was quoted as saying that "Mr. Carnegie's money is as good as any other rich person's and he saw no reason for refusing it." At the end of the meeting, the council approved the ordinance accepting the money and agreeing to Carnegie's conditions.[29] The city agreed to provide suitable sites, but in reality, neighborhood groups were expected to find land, buy it, and donate it to the city.

At the public hearing, Victor C. Sundberg made a case for the Arlington Hills neighborhood. He was wearing several hats. He represented the East Side in the Minnesota House of Representatives.[30] He was the proprietor of the Payne Avenue drug store which served as "Station B," the East Side's main library transfer station, as noted in Chapter One. He was also active in the East Side Commercial Club, which created the East Side Library Fund Committee to seek donations and to search for available property. This committee included many Payne Avenue retailers and professionals, as well as the wives of some of them. The chair of the committee was John L. Schweitz, a 29-year-old mailman who lived with his wife and four children just two blocks away from where the Arlington Hills branch would eventually be built.[31]

Victor Sundberg, the East Side druggist, as pictured in souvenir booklet for the 1906 Payne Avenue Carnival and Street Fair, organized by the East Side Commercial Club.

By November, the committee produced a fundraising letter on its own stationery which announced to the community that "at last, the East Side has hope of realizing a long-desired ambition, that of owning a branch library containing a worthy collection of books and housed in a suitable building." The letter explained that to take advantage of the gift of Andrew Carnegie, referred to as "the Library Builder," the community had to raise $4,000 to buy a suitable property. The letter alerted the recipient that they would be approached during Library Week, November 15 to 21, and asked for a generous donation "for your own sake, for the uplift of the community and particularly because of the value this shall be to our children."[32]

The fundraising efforts were also supported by the Monday Literary Club, which was the women's auxiliary of the East Side Commercial Club and a member of the statewide federation of women's clubs. The goals of the club were self-improvement through study, civic improvement of the community, and "sunshine" work, which included acts of charity. In November, the group passed a resolution stating that the club would "stand by and assist in every way possible the getting a library for the East Side."[33] The meetings of the Monday Literary Club featured papers read on various topics by members, one of whom was Mary Louise Burnquist, the wife of Joseph Burnquist, a lawyer who was elected Lieutenant Governor in 1912 and became governor when Governor Winfield Hammond died in office at the end of 1915. In that same year, Mrs. Burnquist served as president of the Monday Literary Club. In those years, the Burnquists lived at the corner of Burr Avenue and Magnolia Avenue, about five blocks west of Payne Avenue.

The East Side Library Fund Committee reported that they had raised $300 on the first day of Library Week. They used that money to secure a sixty-day option to buy property on Greenbrier, a residential street one block east of Payne Avenue.[34] The committee focused on three lots at the corner of Greenbrier and Jessamine which together provided a 125-foot frontage on Greenbrier and 120 feet along Jessamine. These lots, which were vacant, may have been chosen because they were affordable, but also because the "Payne Avenue" streetcar made its way north from downtown by turning right on York and then north on Greenbrier passing by the library site.[35] Fundraising might have proved more difficult than expected because, by April 1915, the committee had only been able to purchase two of the lots when all three were needed for the proposed building.[36] Eventually, the committee purchased the third lot, and the project went forward.

Designing the Carnegie Branches

While the neighborhoods secured sites, Charles A. Hausler, the City Architect, worked on designs for the three branch libraries. Born in 1889, he had grown up in St. Paul and attended Mechanic Arts School for a few years before dropping out. He then apprenticed for several of the top architects in the Midwest, including Clarence Johnston in St. Paul, Harry Wild Jones in Minneapolis, and Louis Sullivan in Chicago. This was all before he was 21, by which time he had returned to St. Paul and opened his own office, partnering with a number of young, talented architects. The city created the position of City Architect in 1914, and Hausler, who was only 25, was the first person to hold the position.[37]

One of his first duties was overseeing the construction of the main branch of the library on Rice Park. Electus Litchfield of Boston designed the building, and it was Hausler's job to make sure the building was constructed according to plan. A few months after he was appointed, Hausler inspected the building site and determined that the contractor was using substandard bricks in the walls. He ordered the contractor to replace them. The contractor went to the mayor to demand that Hausler be fired, claiming that he was "inexperienced and unqualified." The city stood by the young architect, and the contractor agreed to remove the questionable bricks from the building site.[38] Hausler saw the construction of the new library through to its completion.

Meanwhile, he set to work on producing designs for the three branch libraries that would pass muster with James Bertram. Although he was proficient at a variety of styles, it was almost inevitable that the branch libraries would have a classical appearance. The United States, after all, was in the grip of the Classical Revival in architecture which had been jump-started by the World's Columbian Exposition in 1893. Led by city planner Daniel Burnham, architects from across the country built the "White City" on Chicago's waterfront, a theme park of exposition halls, pavilions, and gardens, designed to promote a return to the symmetry of classic Greek and Roman forms. The inspiration was the Ecole des Beaux-Arts, the Parisian architectural school which championed the order and beauty of classical architecture. Many of the architects who created the buildings on Burnham's grand concourses were alumni. They believed that Greek and Roman models not only expressed order and beauty but democracy as well. For them, the classical revival was the true path to a distinctively American architecture.

Not everyone agreed, most notably Louis Sullivan and those who followed him in the Prairie-style movement, including Frank Lloyd Wright from Wisconsin, and William Gray Purcell and George Grant Elmslie, who practiced together in Minneapolis. These architects thought of their work as a "progressive" rebellion against the Classical Revival. For them, a truly American architecture should be grounded in the uniqueness of the American landscape rather than adapted from European models. Prairie-style architecture made a big splash in the 1910s, but was never able to overcome the dominance

St. Paul Public Library under construction in 1915.

of neo-classical styles, especially in commercial buildings like banks and in public buildings like courthouses and libraries. Architects associated with the Ecole des Beaux-Arts succeeded in making the Classical Revival the dominant style in American architecture.[39]

The Classical Revival, sometimes called Beaux Arts Classicism, was, in fact, a number of closely-related styles. There were Neo-Classical buildings which closely followed Greek and Roman models, with rows of massive columns ornamented with the classical orders. An excellent example in St. Paul is the Union Depot, built in 1923 and restored in 2012. There were Renaissance Revival buildings modeled on Italian Renaissance architecture (which in turn had been based on classical form). A good example is the St. Paul Public Library and James J. Hill Reference Library, the construction of which Hausler was just then overseeing on Rice Park. Finally, there was the Beaux Arts style itself, a more highly ornamented form of the classical revival, of which the recently restored Minnesota State Capital provides a stunning example.

St. Paul Public Library and James J. Hill Reference Library shortly after construction.

The Classical Revival exploded just as public library building surged. We can see the result in many of the great public libraries still in use today, such as the Beaux Arts-styled New York Public Library or the Renaissance Revival-styled Boston Public Library. Many towns and cities built their Carnegie-financed libraries between 1899 and 1919 in some form of Classical Revival style. Today, small-town Minnesota libraries with classical features are often assumed to be "Carnegie libraries," but there were classically-styled libraries that were not funded by Carnegie—such as the Winona Public Library—and there are Carnegie libraries in other styles, including Prairie—such as the Detroit Lakes and Chatfield libraries, or Tudor Revival—such as the Sumner Branch library in Minneapolis, or Arts and Crafts—such as the Little Falls library.

Charles Hausler was a talented architect who worked both sides of the street. He had apprenticed with Louis Sullivan and worked confidently in the Prairie Style. On the other hand, he tended toward the classical in his public buildings, especially the schools he designed for St. Paul. Hausler may have been influenced by the fact that he was, at the same time, overseeing the construction of the Classical Revival main library on Rice Park. Although he might have gone against the grain and designed a library in Prairie or some other style, the young architect opted to design the branch libraries in a classical style. This didn't mean, however, that all three libraries would look the same.

Hausler had just completed plans for the three branch libraries when the Market Hall burned down in April 1915, destroying most of the records of the St. Paul Public Library. His original plans were apparently lost in the fire, but fortunately, the city had a copy in another location. In June, William Dawson Johnston sent two different sets of plans to Bertram, one which featured a mezzanine and one which did not, expecting Bertram to pick one.[40] Bertram returned both sets, informing Johnston that "we do not wish to choose for you." Send your final choice, he said, and we will comment. But he could not resist adding some comments. He didn't like the fact that the main floor had 18-foot ceilings, and the basement only 9-foot ceilings. "You will have more people in the lecture hall [in the basement] than you will ever have on the main floor at one time." He also didn't like the idea of putting the boiler and toilets in a rear wing (they should be in the basement). And finally, at least one of the exteriors, probably Arlington Hills, was too ornate.[41] The negotiations had begun, with Bertram playing the role of a somewhat passive-aggressive critic.

Johnston passed this on to Hausler, who went back to the drawing board. He produced revised plans, but Bertram now felt that the entrance was too wide and that an open space between the door and the circulation desk was too wasteful. In August, Johnston sent a third set of plans to Bertram, "revised in accordance with your instructions."[42] In reply, Bertram told Johnston that "you should not refer to our letters as instructions as we do not wish to force anything on any community."[43] Be that as it may, Hausler followed most of Bertram's "instructions," although he held out for 18-foot-high ceilings, which he argued, worked better given the width and length of the buildings.[44] In the end, Bertram did not press this objection.

Bertram authorized the funding of each branch after he had approved the plans and had Johnston's assurance that the city owned the site and was ready to build. He approved construction of the St. Anthony Park branch on September 8, 1915, the West Side branch (later called Riverview) on November 19, 1915, and the Arlington Hills branch on January 11, 1916. Bertram made clear that the total cost for each building, complete and ready to occupy, could not exceed $25,000.

The city considered the construction of the three libraries to be a single project and opened bids at the end of March 1916. The contract went to Cameron & Co., a St. Paul builder, who took out a building permit for the Arlington Hills library on May 31, 1916. The buildings were substantially complete by the end of the next summer. The St. Anthony Park library opened in July 1917, and the other two in September 1917.

The Neoclassical Palace on Greenbrier

The three libraries that Hausler designed were very similar in their basic shape and layout. Each was a rectangular building with an 80-foot front façade and 40-foot sides. Each had a main floor which was between five and six feet above grade and entered by a central doorway reached by a stairway. As shown in Hausler's original plan for the Arlington Hills first floor, visitors passed through an internal vestibule and came face to face with the circulation desk. One half of

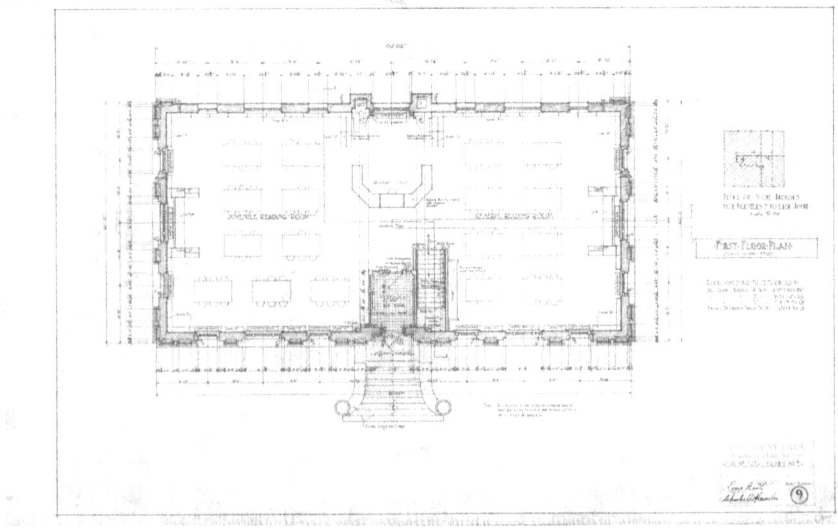

Hausler's plans for the first floor of the Arlington Hills library. The children's department is on the left and the adult reading room on the right.

the main floor was a reading room for adults, and the other half set aside for children. The basements had a lecture hall in one half, and a children's story room, a staff room, toilets, and a boiler room in the other.

Although the buildings had identical footprints, Hausler worked to create exteriors that would make each building unique. One factor which influenced his choices was the site for each building. The Arlington Hills and Riverview branches are on rectangular corner lots in residential areas. As a result, the stairway to the main entrances runs perpendicular to the front façade. In the Riverview building, the stairs are connected by a short concrete walkway to the public sidewalk which runs parallel to the front of the building. The Arlington Hills building is on a deeper lot and is therefore set back farther from the street than the Riverview building. Its stairway descends from the main entrance to a concrete plaza which leads to another set of stairs down to the public sidewalk running parallel to the building. The St. Anthony Park branch, on the other hand, is on a triangular piece of land formed by the diagonal intersection of Como and Carter Avenues. The building is set back about 100 feet from the intersection. The front entrance is reached by a concrete walkway

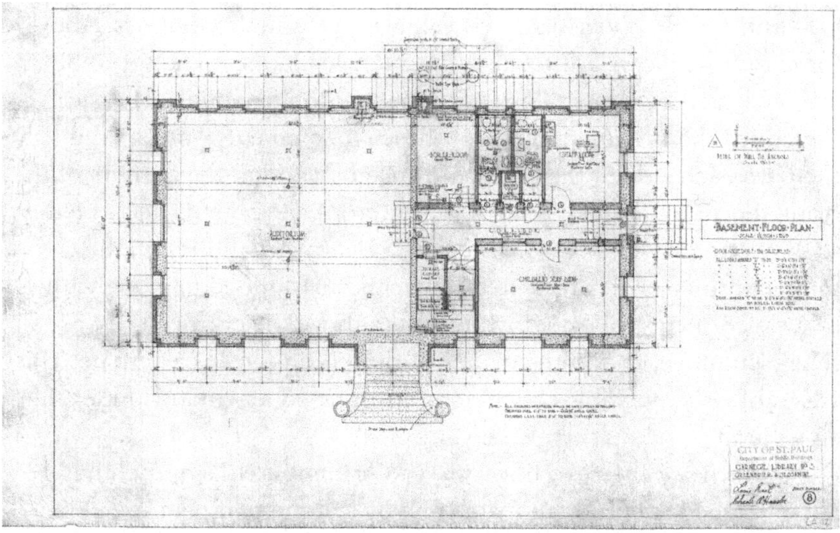

Hausler's plans for the basement of the Arlington Hills Public Library with the auditorium on the left.

running parallel to the front façade which links the public sidewalks on Carter and Como. Each of these walkways leads to stairways which are parallel to the front of the building. The two stairways meet at a small porch in front of the main door.

A fundamental characteristic of classical style is symmetry, and all three buildings have primary facades which are strictly symmetrical. Each is built on a stone base which supports elevations built of dark brown brick with limestone trim. The front façades are all organized around seven bays, with the front door in the central bay and the other six holding windows. In the St. Anthony Park and Riverview branches, all seven bays are topped by identical rounded arches made of brick. In these libraries, the bays are separated by brick pilasters. The seven linked arches echo the Renaissance Revival styling of the seven arches between the two main entrances of the St. Paul Public Library on Rice Park.

In the design of the Arlington Hills branch, Hausler turned to a restrained Beaux Arts approach which resulted in a building which is more highly ornamented than its two siblings. Here the seven bays are not identical, although the rule of strict symmetry is preserved. The second and sixth bays have large stone arches holding arched windows similar to the other two libraries, and the fourth (center) bay houses the entrance which is also topped by a stone arch. The first, third, fifth, and seventh bays have rectangular windows. Above these four windows are rectangular marble plaques. The seven bays are separated by stone pilasters topped by Ionic capitals. Hausler magnified the ornamental use of these stone pilasters by pairing them on each side of the main entrance bay and at the corners of the front and side facades. As a result, the front elevation is decorated with twelve pilasters. As is typical of a Beaux Arts building, the main entrance is ornate. The doorway is surrounded in stone with a stone cornice supported by brackets. Above the cornice is a bas-relief sculpture, and in the center of that, is a marble cartouche. This ensemble is capped by a semicircular multi-pane window under the stone arch.

Unlike the other two libraries, the Arlington Hills branch has a low-pitched roof hidden from view by a stone parapet topped by stone coping. The parapet is about four feet high and is divided into bays by its own short pilasters which echo the pilasters below.

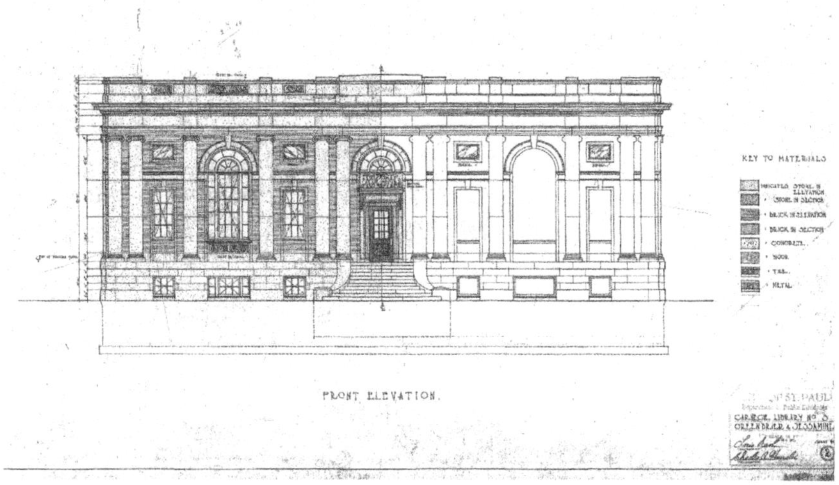

Hausler's original plans for the front elevation of the Arlington Hills library.

The front façade of the Arlington Hills library shortly after construction.

The bays of the parapet are ornamented by grillwork, except for the central bay over the main entrance which rises to a pediment. Between the parapet and the capitals of the pilasters is a classical entablature, with architrave, frieze, and cornice.

All three branch libraries, plus the new downtown library, were formally dedicated during Library Week, October 3 through 14, 1917, with each library having its celebration on a different date. The dedication of the Arlington Hills branch came on Saturday, October 13. It was an all-day event sponsored by the East Side Commercial Club and organized by a committee led by Representative Victor Sundberg which also included Louis Swenson, the president of the club. The plan was to have an open house in the afternoon with music by the orchestras of Johnson High School and Phalen Park grade school, and a reception in the evening at which Governor Burnquist and head librarian William Dawson Johnston, would speak. Burnquist apparently did not appear, but a large crowd filled the new building that evening to hear Johnston formally inaugurate the new building and to be entertained by a number of East Side musicians.[45]

This event marked the reinvention of the library. Arlington Hills and two other communities now had neighborhood libraries housed in impressive buildings designed to clearly announce the dignity and importance of what went on inside their walls. Soon, other neighborhoods would succeed in their campaigns for a local branch library. No longer would working people have to make the long trip downtown to use the library after a hard day's work, as the *Minnesota Union Advocate* had complained. This reinvention was the result of a great paradox. Andrew Carnegie's wealth had been wrung from the labor of working people. What he had not been willing to give at the bargaining table, he now returned in part by investing in the public good.

A Closer Look...

Charles Hausler

St. Paul's All-Purpose Architect

Over his long career, Charles Hausler had a major impact on the look of St. Paul's neighborhoods, designing hundreds of buildings of all types. In addition to the three Carnegie branch libraries, he designed many schools, churches, and commercial buildings. He also was a prolific designer of homes.

It may come as a surprise to admirers of his libraries that many of his well-known buildings are not related to the Classical Revival. His churches, for example, might be Gothic, Romanesque, or Byzantine Revival, and his homes were often in Craftsman or Prairie Style, including his own home in the West Seventh neighborhood. Adapting to changing times, he had great success designing Art Deco buildings in the 1930s.

His eight-year tenure as City Architect came to an end in 1922 when he was elected to the Minnesota Senate. He represented St. Paul in the Senate until 1937, starting out as a progressive Republican and ending up as a member of the Farmer-Labor Party. His architectural practice thrived during these years, and he continued working through the 1950s.

Several of his buildings have been added to the National Register of Historic Places. The list includes the three

Carnegie branch libraries; St. Mary's Catholic Church in Hague, North Dakota—a Romanesque Revival building with Byzantine touches, which he designed for a German-Russian parish that had lost its original church to fire; and two Art Deco buildings—the Minnesota Building in downtown St. Paul and the Minnesota Milk Company Building on University Avenue.

Examples of Hausler's school designs can be seen in the Como Park Elementary School at 730 Wheelock Parkway West and the Randolph Heights Elementary School at 348 Hamline.

For a sampling of his Prairie style home designs, drive by the homes at 1058 St. Clair in Summit Hill, 633 Holly in Summit-University, or 449 Arbor in West Seventh.

Hausler also used Prairie style effectively to create structures for St. Paul parks, including Como Park and Phalen Park. One that survives is the pavilion in St. Paul's Mounds Park, which still shelters picnickers a century after its construction.

A Closer Look...

The Three Carnegies

Charles Hausler designed the three libraries with the same floor plans and dimensions. All were expressions of the Classical Revival style. Like any creative architect, however, he was not content to design three identical buildings. They were siblings, but not triplets.

Riverview Public Library

St. Anthony Park Public Library

Arlington Hills Public Library

The front elevations of the Riverview and St. Anthony Park libraries are organized around seven identical arched openings. The have hipped roofs with overhanging eaves ornamented by modillions. The Arlington Hills branch has a more varied front façade which features a series of classical pilasters. It is also distinguished by its low slope roof hidden by a stone parapet. The first two are expressions of the Renaissance Revival wing of the Classical Revival, while the third reflects the Beaux Arts approach.

Which design do you think was most successful?

- Chapter 2 Endnotes -

[1] Charles Ames to Henry Pritchett, March 3, 1914. Carnegie Corporation of New York Records, Columbia University Libraries, Series II Files on Microfilm, Part A.1 Libraries, Reel 27. All correspondence with Bertram is on Reel 27.

[2] James Bertram to Charles Ames, March 25, 1914.

[3] Charles Ames to James Bertram, April 2, 1914.

[4] James Bertram to Charles Ames, April 6, 1914

[5] E. A. Young, President of the Board of Library Directors and Mayor Herbert Keller to James Bertram, May 1, 1914.

[6] James Bertram to Charles Ames, May 8, 1914.

[7] "Carnegie Plans $75,000 Gift to Libraries Here," *St. Paul Dispatch,* May 16, 1914, p. 1.

[8] David Nasaw, *Andrew Carnegie* (New York: Penguin, 2006), p. 386–448. Carnegie was in Scotland during the Homestead strike and after the fact claimed that the violence would not have happened if he, rather than Frick, had been on the scene. Nasaw makes clear, however, that Frick acted with Carnegie's full knowledge and approval.

[9] Durand R. Miller, *Carnegie Grants for Library Buildings 1890–1917* (New York: Carnegie Corporation, 1943); George S. Bobinski, *Carnegie Libraries: Their History and Impact on American Public Library Development* (Chicago: American Library Association, 1969), p.3–24; Theodore Jones, *Carnegie Libraries across America: A Public Legacy* (New York: Wiley and Sons, 1997), p. 25–37. Abigail A. Van Slyck, *Free to All: Carnegie Libraries and American Culture 1890–1920* (Chicago: University of Chicago Press, 1995), p. 19–27; Joseph Frazier Wall, *Andrew Carnegie* (New York: Oxford U. Press, 1970), p 808–819; Nasaw, p. 605–607.

[10] Kevin Clemens, *Carnegie Libraries in Minnesota* (Lake Elmo: Demontreville Press, 2011), 12.

[11] Andrew Carnegie, *The Gospel of Wealthy and other Timely Essays* (Cambridge: Harvard University Press, 1962), p. 25; Wall, p. 806–817.

[12] Carnegie, p. 29.

[13] Carnegie, p. 36.

[14] Andrew Carnegie, *Autobiography of Andrew Carnegie* (Boston: Houghton Mifflin, 1920), p. 45–46.

[15] Bobinski, p. 166. Carnegie's requirement that a city spend 10 percent of the total cost of the library on yearly maintenance failed to take the inflation of maintenance costs into account.

[16] Bobinski, p. 34–56.

[17] Bruce Colwell, *Everlasting Influences: The Centennial History of the Northfield Carnegie Public Library 1910–2010* (Northfield: Northfield Public Library, 2010), p. 14–15.

[18] Clemens, p. 121–122. See also Durand R. Miller, *Carnegie Grants for Library Buildings, 1890–1917* (New York: Carnegie Corporation, 1943). This grant to Duluth was in addition to the 1899 grant for the downtown library.

[19] Bertram revised the pamphlet several times. The text for the 1915 version is reprinted in Van Slyck, p 221–223 and the floor plans at p. 38–39.

[20] Bobinski, p. 63.

[21] Bobinski, p. 62.

[22] Van Slyck, p. 223.

[23] "Build Our Own Libraries," [editorial], *St. Paul Dispatch,* May 18, 1914, p. 10.

[24] Bobinski, p. 89–94.

[25] "Trades and labor Assembly Elects New Set of Officers," *Labor Review,* July 19, 1912, p. 1.

[26] "Library Needs Hale Bequest," *Minnesota Union Advocate,* November 3, 1916, p. 4.

[27] "Park Seeks First Library: North St. Anthony Community Gets Ear of Commissioner Yoerg in Scheme," *St. Paul Dispatch,* July 7, 1914, p. 14.

[28] "3 Libraries Near for St. Paul," *St. Paul Dispatch,* July 23, 1914, p. 9.

[29] "Libraries: Johnston Shows Need," *St. Paul Dispatch,* July 31, 1914, p. 2. Johnston forwarded a certified copy of the ordinance to James Bertram. Johnston to Bertram, August 31, 1914.

[30] Sundberg served one term as the District 33 member in the Minnesota House of Representatives during the 38th Legislative Session (1913–1914).

[31] "The Arlington Branch Library," *The Library Beacon, St. Paul Public Library,* Vol IV, Number 8 (December 1932). Schweitz later was president of the Polish-American Club. Personal information from Schweitz's World War I draft registration card and from the 1920 Census.

[32] Letter dated November 10, 1914 in the archives of the Arlington Hills Public Library.

[33] Minutes for November 2, 1914, *Secretary's Record Books, Volume 1: 1910–1921,* Monday Literary Club, St. Paul. Available at the archives of the Minnesota Historical Society.

[34] "Library Fund Growing," *St. Paul Dispatch,* November 17, 1914, p. 1.

[35] The Payne line continued north to Maryland where it headed east to Kenard Avenue. John W. Diers, *Twin Cities by Trolley* (Minneapolis: University of Minnesota Press, 2007), p. 276–277.

[36] "3 Branch Library Plans are Ready: Will Not Sent to Carnegie Managers until Approval of Sites," *St. Paul Dispatch,* April 2, 1915, p. 11.

[37] Alan Lathrop, *Minnesota Architects,* p. 94–95; Jeffrey Hess and Paul Larson, *St. Paul's Architecture: A History* (Minneapolis: University of Minnesota Press, 2006), p. 96–100.

[38] "Confirm Report of Attack on Hausler," *St. Paul Pioneer Press,* August 24, 1914, p. 10.

[39] The contest between these competing visions is well told in John Burchard and Albert Bush-Brown, *The Architecture of America: A Social and Cultural History,* Abridged Edition (Boston: Little, Brown, 1966), p. 139–235.

[40] William Dawson Johnston to James Bertram, June 18, 1915.

[41] James Bertram to William Dawson Johnston, June 29, 1915. An undated early sketch of the Arlington Hills library shows a more ornate façade and a hipped roof surrounded by a classical balustrade. In the materials of the St. Paul Public Library in the archives at the Minnesota Historical Society.

[42] William Dawson Johnston to James Bertram, August 17, 1915

[43] James Bertram to William Dawson Johnston, August 23, 1915.

[44] William Dawson Johnston to James Bertram, November 16, 1915.

[45] "Crowd Sees Library," *St. Paul Daily News,* October 14, 1917, p. 3.

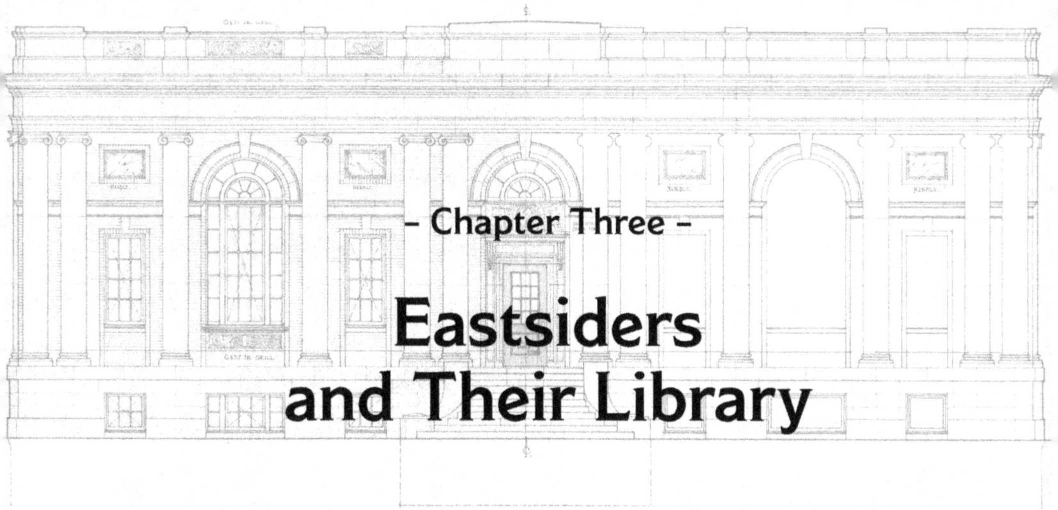

– Chapter Three –

Eastsiders and Their Library

In the "souvenir" booklet celebrating their 1906 Carnival and Street Fair, the East Side Commercial Club noted that "the First Ward," as they often called the East Side in those days, was separated from the rest of the city by railroads, and therefore was "somewhat individual and self-contained." The club, composed mostly of Payne Avenue shopkeepers and professionals of Scandinavian ancestry, boasted that the local population had built the East Side "into a city of their own, containing more than thirty thousand people, where every convenience and product of modern civilization can be found." They went on to brag about their local schools, their handsome churches, their freedom from vice, and the educated independence of the voters, which referred, of course, only to the men of the community.[1] What this city-within-a-city lacked was a library. The East Side Commercial Club took the lead in filling this gap. When it opened in 1917, the Arlington Hills Public Library was a response to the popular demand for books, magazines, and a place to read and learn.

By 1906, the East Side was a thriving community with a well-developed sense of its own unique identity, even though the neighborhood was still quite young. Just thirty years earlier, there were no businesses on Payne Avenue, and the residential blocks were just being divided into lots. Those were the years of the great European migration to the United States and cities were expanding quickly. The greater East Side was settled by Swedish, Irish, and German immigrants, but it was the Swedes who formed the most cohesive community in the early days. By 1900, these groups were joined by immigrants from Italy, Poland, and other Eastern European countries. After World War I, they were joined by immigrants from Mexico, as well as Mexican-Americans and African-Americans who migrated from the southern states. The ethnic mix of the neighborhood kept evolving and would continue to evolve after World War II, but the library was always there, open to each group of new arrivals.

Up from Swede Hollow to Arlington Hills

The East Side's identity as its own unique place is grounded in geography, particularly the way the Mississippi River developed over the millennia. From Minneapolis, the river flows directly south until it reaches its confluence with the Minnesota River near Mendota. The Dakota call this place *Bdote* ("the place where the two waters come together") and consider it the center of the world and the place of their origins as a people.[2] The Mississippi then makes a sharp left turn and flows northeast to the spot where Trout Brook and Phalen creeks once came together and flowed into it from the north. At that point, it makes another sharp turn, this one to the south. Those two streams reached the Mississippi through a break in the sandstone cliffs created by an ancient, earlier version of the river. This opening in the cliff wall allowed easy access to the river. The Dakota gathered there for fishing and ceremonies, just upstream from the massive burial mounds in what is commonly called Indian Mounds Regional Park today.

The European settlers were also attracted to the spot and built a road down to the river landing, just east of where downtown St. Paul would eventually develop on the heights. Trout Brook ran south to the river on a path similar to present day I-35E, and Phalen Creek ran southwest to the river from its source at Lake Phalen. The settlers built mills to harness the water power below the confluence of the two streams. Later, these creek beds provided natural corridors for the railroads, leading to the tracks, switching yards and repair shop yards which formed the western and southern borders of the East Side and provided job opportunities for the first wave of immigrants.[3]

Above its junction with Trout Brook, Phalen Creek flowed through a deep ravine about three-quarters of a mile long. This area became the home of several waves of immigrants, but took its name, *Svenska Dalen,* or Swede Hollow, from the first group to build simple wood-framed houses there and call it home. From the beginning, it

Swede Hollow, with the Hamm's Brewery in the center background and Jacob Hamm's mansion high on the bluff to the right.

functioned as a "stepping stone" neighborhood, a place where new arrivals could find or build cheap housing until they could move up, metaphorically and literally.

Although many Swedes settled in rural areas, more than half of all Swedish immigrants to the United States ended up in places like Chicago, Minneapolis, and St. Paul. Minnesota had the largest Swedish population, peaking at about 126,000 in 1905, and a good portion lived in the Twin Cities. Like most immigrants, they came for jobs—and the railroads, lumber mills, flour mills, slaughterhouses, construction firms, cabinet shops, garment factories, and breweries needed both skilled and unskilled workers in those years. Eventually, Swedes made up 7.5 percent of the population of the Twin Cities, which made it possible for them to create their own distinct neighborhoods.[4]

In St. Paul, those neighborhoods were primarily on the East Side. In the 1870s, most Swedes started in Swede Hollow and then moved to Railroad Island, the nearby triangular area of lower Payne Avenue so called because railroad tracks surrounded it. As unskilled Swedish workers acquired trades and other skills, they moved up Payne Avenue to Arlington Hills, which was subdivided by real estate speculators into a typical grid pattern in 1873. Those who could afford it bought a lot and hired a contractor to build a "pattern book" house which might be a four-square, a bungalow, a Cape Cod, or a duplex, sheathed in weatherboard or stucco. By the turn of the century, the neighborhood was also home to prosperous retailers and professionals who built more substantial Italianate and Queen Anne homes. The majority were skilled workers and laborers employed by the railroads, Hamm's Brewing, and later, at 3M, Seeger Refrigerator (which later merged with Whirlpool), and other local manufacturing firms.[5]

Commercial districts developed along Payne Avenue and Arcade Street, two north-south streets that ran parallel to each other and four blocks apart. However, it was Payne Avenue, that became the "main street" of the East Side. By 1885, upper Payne Avenue was a lively commercial street on which most of the property owners and merchants had Swedish surnames. There were groceries, meat shops, shoe and boot stores, confectionery stores, drug stores, furniture stores, dry good stores, undertakers, and many others. Starting in 1905, Swedish immigrants opened banks on Payne Avenue, and in 1923, two of them merged and built the Payne Avenue State Bank at 965 Payne. This Beaux Arts structure housed the bank on the first

Eastsiders outside the original Payne Avenue State Bank shortly before it moved into its new building in 1923.

The bank is gone but the Payne Avenue State Bank building still stands at 965 Payne Avenue.

floor and provided nine, second-floor offices for East Side physicians and dentists. The building still stands at the corner of Payne and Case and was added to the National Register of Historic Places in 2007.[6]

Payne Avenue was also central to the social and cultural life of the community. In 1909, the Palm Theater was built at 999 Payne as a venue for both music and films. In 1915, the movie house known first as the Venus Theater and later as the Capitol Theater debuted at 1077 Payne. The neighborhood also had its own newspapers, including the *East St. Paul Examiner* (1919-1921) and the *East Side Journal* (1922-1938), which provided news for the community and advertising for the merchants. The carnival and street fair which the East Side Commercial Club began in 1906, eventually evolved into the Harvest Festival held every September.[7]

In 1916, the neighborhood was connected to downtown by the streetcar line built by the Twin Cities Rapid Transit Company. The line came up lower Payne Avenue to York Street, and then jogged one block east and continued north on Greenbrier to Maryland because the residential street offered a gentler grade than Payne Avenue.[8] As a result, the streetcar passed the front door of the Arlington Hills Public Library.

Payne Avenue in the 1920s.

Dr. Robert Earl, a physician and entrepreneur, was a leader of this energetic and ambitious business community. The son of Swedish immigrants, he started a medical practice on Payne Avenue in 1897, and in 1900, built a commercial building at 881 Payne which housed his practice and for a while, his home. Dr. Earl also founded two of the early banks on the avenue and later the Mounds Park Sanitarium, which became the Mounds Park Hospital. He eventually left the neighborhood and moved to Summit Avenue, St. Paul's wealthiest neighborhood, setting an early example that would be followed by other successful businessmen.

One of the first tenants in Dr. Earl's new building was the Bodin Drug Store, a partnership formed in 1896 by John Bodin and Victor Sundberg. When Earl opened his new building at 881 Payne, Bodin and Sundberg moved their drugstore there from 856 Payne and expanded it to feature "imported Scandinavian remedies." In 1906, Bodin and Sundberg agreed to host Station B, one of the St. Paul library's first transfer stations. When John Bodin died a few years later, Sundberg continued his partnership with Helen Bodin, John's widow.[9] Eventually, the firm had three East Side drug stores, and its Payne Avenue store moved to 896 Payne, where it continued to be the location of Station B. Sundberg was an official of the East Side

Nils Nelson ready to set a column on its pedestal during the construction of the State Capitol.

Commercial Club and played a leading role in the establishment of the Arlington Hills Public Library.[10]

A more typical representative of the Arlington Hills neighborhood was Nils Nelson, a highly skilled stonemason who played a major role in the construction of the state capitol. Born in Sweden, he came to Chicago in the 1880s and worked in construction. By the 1890s, he was married and settled in St. Paul's East Side, owning a home at 1107 Payne Avenue. He worked for Butler-Ryan Company (later Butler Brothers Company), which had the contract for the stone work in the Minnesota Capitol which was built between 1896 and 1905. As head stonemason for the project, the tall, red-haired, bushy-bearded Swede supervised the laying of most of the marble on the exterior facades. The confident, highly-skilled craftsman was also president of the local stonemasons' union. During the construction of the capitol, he faced down Cass Gilbert, the project's famous architect, who had questioned his approach to hoisting large columns into place. Gilbert wanted Nelson fired, but the Butlers could hardly afford to lose their head mason. After Gilbert went back to his office in New York, Nelson was back on the job. Years later, Nelson tried to return to the State Capitol as a legislator. In 1918, by this time in his 50s, he ran for the Minnesota House seat for the East Side district. He lost a close race to another Swede. Meanwhile, Nelson kept working, usually as a self-employed contractor, and also built a three-story brick building on Payne Avenue which became the home of the Montgomery Lodge of Free Masons of which he was a member.[11]

Governor Burnquist focused his 1918 campaign on the alleged disloyalty of the Non-Partisan League and its candidate Charles A. Lindbergh, Sr.

Another member of the Arlington Heights Swedish community was Joseph Burnquist, a lawyer who was elected Lieutenant Governor in 1912 and became governor when Governor Winfield Hammond died at the end of 1915. In 1916, he ran as an incumbent and retained the office in a landslide. Burnquist had attended Carleton College and then earned a law degree at the University of Minnesota. In about 1905, he and his wife settled in the East Side while he began a law practice in the Endicott Building downtown. In 1911, the family built the Queen Anne house which still sits at the corner of Burr and Magnolia, about five blocks west of Payne.[12]

Burnquist was elected to the Minnesota House of Representatives in 1908 from an East Side district. In the legislature, he earned a reputation as a strong progressive. Later, however, he moved to the right and aligned himself with business-oriented Republicans like Senator Knute Nelson. In 1916, he angered the labor movement by openly favoring management in the miners' strike on the Iron Range, particularly by his policy of encouraging the local sheriff to deputize private mine guards as peace officers.[13] When World War I broke out, the legislature created the Minnesota Commission of Public Safety (MCPS) to govern the state during the war. The commission included Burnquist, the Attorney General, and five members appointed by Burnquist. All but one were conservative businessmen. The MCPS was intolerant of any expression of German culture and opposed to union organizing of any kind.[14]

With good cause, the trade union and immigrant communities, especially the Germans but also many Scandinavians, were angered by the policies of the MCPS. This may have been why Governor Burnquist did not make his anticipated appearance at the opening of the Arlington Hills Public Library in September 1917, although to be sure, the war years were busy times. In 1918, the Non-Partisan League nominated Charles Lindbergh, Sr., a steadfast progressive who had served several terms in Congress, to challenge Burnquist in the Republican primary for governor. With a great deal of help from the MCPS, Burnquist ran a "loyalty" campaign, painting Lindbergh as a traitor because he had questioned the decision to enter the European war. The MCPS also made it very difficult for Lindbergh to campaign in many counties. Burnquist won the primary with about

57 percent of the vote statewide, but in the First Ward, Lindbergh won 55 percent of the vote.[15]

Charles A. Lindbergh, Sr, the Non-Partisan League candidate for governor in the 1918 Republican Primary.

Burnquist's poor showing on his home turf was perhaps an indication of the growing anger among immigrants and trade unionists at the rightward drift of the Republican Party, especially during the war. It also reflected the growth of a class consciousness in the working-class district, moving past generations of ethnic identification. The fact that urban workers in the First Ward were willing to vote for the candidate of the NPL, which was, after all, a party of farmers, indicates that the political coalition that would in a few years lead to the Farmer-Labor Party was beginning to take shape. In 1932, the East Side would help elect William Mahoney, a Farmer-Labor leader and editor of the St. Paul *Union Advocate,* to become mayor of St. Paul, the same year that Floyd B. Olson became the first Farmer-Labor governor of the state.

Although Swedes were the largest group on the East Side and Swedish merchants and professionals continued to dominate upper Payne Avenue into the 1950s, new groups of immigrants continued to arrive. At first, they built their own institutions, but in time, they organized with their neighborhoods from other communities. In 1881, just as many Swedes were moving out of Swede Hollow, part of it became known as "Connemara Patch," a small Irish community. These Irish families from Connemara in County Galway, Ireland, had been sponsored by John Ireland, the Catholic bishop of St. Paul, who helped them settle in Big Stone County in western Minnesota. As most of the men had been engaged in fishing in Ireland, they fared poorly as rookie farmers out on the prairie. When they faced destitution in their first winter, Bishop Ireland found them jobs in the St. Paul railroads, and they moved into Swede Hollow.[16]

By the turn of the century, Italian was the most common language in Swede Hollow, which became one of the two distinct Italian neighborhoods in St. Paul, the other being on the Upper Levee under the High Bridge. The Italian men tended to work for the railroads or at Hamm's Brewery. Eventually, the Italians moved up into Railroad Island, just west of the ravine. Soon the lower portion of Payne Avenue which ran through this area became a "Little Italy" commercial district with saloons, groceries, and restaurants. This community campaigned for its own Catholic parish, and in 1911, Bishop Ireland finally agreed, leading to the construction of St. Ambrose, the only Italian national parish in Minnesota. In that same year, the Guild of Catholic Women created the Christ Child Center, a social settlement house for the Italian immigrant community. It had a gymnasium, auditorium, library, and clinics, but was known in the community as *la Scuola* because of the citizenship classes held there.[17]

After the turn of the century, Poles also settled in the East End in numbers similar to the Italians. The center of this community was the Church of St. Casimir at 937 E. Jessamine, built by the Catholic Church in 1904 to serve the growing Polish community on the East Side. It was added to the National Register of Historic Places in 1983. In 1911, several Polish-American organizations came together to build Pulaski Hall, "the Polish Home," on Arcade Street. In 1928, the Polish American Club was organized to provide a unified voice for the community and to maintain and expand Pulaski Hall.

Church of St. Casimir

John L. Schweitz, a leading member of the Polish community, chaired the committee that, in 1915, raised funds to purchase the lots for the Arlington Hills Public Library. When the Polish American Club was organized in 1928, he was elected first vice president. He also edited the monthly newsletter of the club. Although John Schweitz worked for the post office most of his life, the Schweitz family name was best known on the East Side for their liquor stores and saloons, especially Schweitz Bar at 956 Payne.[18]

Meanwhile, new immigrants were making the East Side their home. In the 1920s, Mexicans began arriving in St. Paul, primarily on the West Side, but some also on the East Side. They came for seasonal agricultural work, but a few stayed, settling in various East Side neighborhoods including Swede Hollow, which after World War II was primarily a Mexican enclave. To these new residents, the ravine with its steep sides was no longer "Swede Hollow" but "El Pozo" (the well). Like the other immigrant communities, life revolved around a church, in this case, a chapel housed in a reconstructed boxcar.[19]

What the Library Offered

From the beginning, the immigrant communities of the East Side have responded enthusiastically to the reinvention of the library as a neighborhood institution. It became one of the places where people from different backgrounds came together. The new library was overwhelmed by a surge of visitors when it opened in September 1917. According to news reports, the library "has had such a large patronage that every second day it was necessary to send to the main library building for additional supplies of books because the shelves were empty."[20] Although it was only open for the last four months of 1917, its circulation for the year was 26,000 even though its book collection had only reached 4,225 by the end of the year. This represented a "turnover" rate of about 6, meaning that on average, each book was loaned 6 times during that short period. In 1918, its first full year of operation, its book collection had grown to almost 7,000, and its circulation was just under 70,000.

The construction of the three branch libraries, along with the many delivery stations that the St. Paul library continued to maintain, contributed to a massive growth in the overall number of

Maryland Ave
Grrenbrier Ave
Rose St
Geranium St
Nils Nelson Home
St Casimir Church
Jessamine St
Magnolia St
Arlington Hills Public Library
Joseph Burnquist Home
Cook St
Lawson St
Payne Ave
PAYNE AVE BUSINESS DISTRICT
Jenks St
Pulaski Hall
Payne Ave State Bank
Case Ave
Arcade St
N Forest St
Schweitz Bar
Sims St
Arkwright St
Burr St
Edgerton St
York St
Bodin's Drug
Seeger Refrigerator, later Whirlpool
Hamm's Brewery
Minnehaha St
St Ambrose Church
3M
RAILROAD ISLAND
SWEDE HOLLOW
Lafayette Ave
E Seventh St
E Sixth St
Maria Ave
E Third St
DAYTON'S BLUFF
DOWNTOWN
Mississippi River
St Paul's East Side in the 1920's
Railroad lines
Streetcar lines

books loaned. In 1914, the year that Carnegie approved the gift to St. Paul, the library loaned books 584,000 times, of which about 125,000 were from the delivery stations (21%), 145,000 through the school and playground programs (24%), and the rest, about 314,500, from the central library (54%). By 1918, the first full year that the branches were open, the total circulation had grown to 955,600, with 359,600 (38%) coming from the branches and stations, 258,000 coming from the schools and playgrounds (27%), and about 338,000 coming from the downtown library (35%). System-wide circulation reached 1.5 million in 1925, with the branches and stations contributing 434,700 to the total.[21]

The number of people holding library cards exceeded 71,000 in 1922 as more citizens each year registered for borrowing privileges. In 1922, about 17,000 applied for their first library card, compared to about 12,000 during 1918. In most years, about 55 percent of adult cards were taken out by women and 45 percent by men. The gender breakdown among younger readers was about even. For several years, the library kept records of the occupations of citizens applying for cards. In 1922, about 41 percent of the men reporting an occupation worked in blue collar jobs, including skilled and unskilled workers in manufacturing, transportation, and service occupations (including barbers, janitors, and waiters). Another 41 percent worked in retail trade (store clerks, deliverymen, salesmen) or in clerical occupations (clerks, bookkeepers). The final 18 percent were professionals, including doctors, lawyers, engineers, teachers, and clergymen. Among the women applicants, almost half were office clerks or stenographers, followed closely by teachers, with smaller numbers employed as factory workers (primarily textiles), nurses, social workers, and telephone operators.[22]

A significant number of patrons were foreign-born, and in 1918, for example, about 25 percent of the nearly 12,000 new cards were issued to patrons who listed themselves as immigrants, among whom the largest groups were Germans and Swedes. As a result of the war, the number of immigrants registering for new cards in 1920 declined.

Librarians generally believed that they had a responsibility to help new immigrants become citizens, but they were unsure about exactly what that meant, especially with respect to their book and periodical collections. Would immigrants be more quickly

"Americanized" if they could only find books in English at their local library, or should libraries try to meet the needs of immigrant populations by providing books and periodicals in German, Swedish, Norwegian, Yiddish, Polish, Bohemian, and other languages? Ultimately, libraries did provide materials in languages other than English, and still do, but probably never in the quantity that immigrant communities might desire.

Gratia Countryman, head of the Minneapolis Public Library and one of the country's leading librarians, described how she came to grips with the issue. Writing in 1898, when she was still second in command at the Minneapolis library, she admitted that for many years she had felt "that the purchase of books in foreign languages should be minimized." Then a visit to a branch library changed her mind. She witnessed a group of immigrants receiving new books in their native language, and "they gathered around these treasures like flies around a molasses jug." Were they worse citizens, she asked herself, because the library recognized their particular needs? On the contrary, she concluded, "a cosmopolitan library" with a large foreign-language collection would do more to encourage assimilation than a library which ignored the needs of the immigrant public.[23]

The St. Paul Public Library always had books in languages other than English, but the collection was limited. In 1913, when the library owned about 150,000 books, about 6 percent were in foreign languages, with books in German and Swedish accounting for over half of those. That meant that the library owned only 1,365 books in Swedish. In 1922, the library lent foreign language books over 11,000 times, but that represented less than 1 percent of the total circulation. Across the river, the Minneapolis library was lending many more foreign language books not only because it had more books, but also because it produced pamphlets which listed foreign language holdings and designated particular branches as depositories for foreign language books. With respect to Swedish language books, Minneapolis had a wide selection of contemporary fiction, including novels which many librarians considered less than edifying. The Swedish collection in St. Paul tended to be older, non-fiction tomes.[24] It was difficult to correct this problem, however, since the St. Paul library's budget for purchasing any new books, whatever the language, was shrinking in the 1920s. The Arlington Hills branch did not go out of its way to publicize the availability of Swedish language books. Nevertheless, Laura Killian, an Arlington Hills librarian from 1919 to 1950, recalled that branch had "a good collection" of Swedish books, and in the early years at least, patrons who only read Swedish used them.[25]

Loaning books was not the only way the library connected with the community. Each Carnegie library had a lecture hall in the basement, and these rooms were heavily used by the community. In 1917 and 1918, the auditorium was in almost constant use by Red Cross volunteers doing war work. In 1920 and 1921, "Americanization classes" were regularly held in the auditorium and in 1926, an "English for Foreign Learner" class met 51 times. Other frequent users of the auditorium were the East Side Commercial Club and the Boy Scouts. During the Depression and the war years, however, the auditorium was used infrequently, leading the Arlington Hills librarian to comment in 1945 that "the social life of the people was centered around the churches, of which there are many, particularly Lutheran." She felt that there were few organizations where people intermingled, and she hoped that the newly organized Arlington Hills Library Association would be one of them.[26]

Most likely the Arlington Hills branch's biggest contribution to "Americanization" was its focus on children. Libraries began to recognize and respond to the special needs of children in the 1890s, and by the 1910s, most new libraries were designed to accommodate a separate children's department. In her speech to the Minnesota Library Association conference in 1905, Gratia Countryman celebrated the importance of the children's room of the local library, outfitted with "low tables, picture books, and low shelves containing fairy stories and their favorite authors." She wanted story hours to introduce children to the pleasures of reading. She told her fellow librarians that she hoped that if the library were welcoming, children would "always count it among their friends."[27] As we saw, James Bertram's suggested floor plans for Carnegie libraries called for a separate children's area, and Charles Hausler's designs set aside roughly half of the first floor for children.

In 1918, the combined "juvenile" circulation of the branches and stations was about 199,000 while the adult circulation was only 160,000. In that year, the Arlington Hills branch was the most child-oriented of the branches, with two children's books borrowed for every adult book. On average, each of its juvenile books was loaned 13 times during that year. Not surprisingly, the librarians complained that their books tended to get worn out and needed replacements. By the early 1920s, adults caught up and began borrowing more books than children from the branches, including Arlington Hills.[28] The participation of younger readers was also reflected in the new library cards issued in the years after the branches opened. In 1918, the St. Paul libraries registered almost 12,000 new library cardholders. Of these, about 36 percent were juveniles. In 1922, about 46 percent of the 11,000 new cards went to young readers.[29]

The Arlington Hills librarians worked hard to bring young readers into the library. For one thing, they made outreach to local schools a major priority. In 1918, a former Johnson High School teacher was hired as the assistant librarian with the specific goal of encouraging cooperation with the local school librarians who arranged with teachers to bring their classes to tour the library. By the early 1930s, students from most of the East Side's schools, including Johnson High School, Cleveland Junior High School, and several public and parochial "grade" schools, visited the library.[30] Following Gratia Countryman's advice, the librarians also organized regularly scheduled story hours as a way to attract children even before they were readers. In 1920, the Arlington Hills branch reported 68 story hours in the auditorium, although the Saturday morning story hours were discontinued in 1922, probably as a result of staff cutbacks.

The Challenges of the Interwar Years

Although the Arlington Hills Public Library and its two siblings at St. Anthony Park and Riverview got off to a strong start, the decades between the two world wars were difficult for St. Paul's library system as a whole. William Dawson Johnston, who had been hired in 1914, was an energetic leader who focused on taking library services to the neighborhoods and aggressively publicizing their availability. In 1921, he requested a one-year leave because he had been asked to organize the thousands of books that had been sent to France into a permanent English language library for use by American soldiers in Paris during the war. When the Commissioner of Education, the city council member who oversaw the library, denied his request, he resigned and left for France.[31]

The Commissioner replaced Johnston with Webster Wheelock, a former owner of the *St. Paul Pioneer Press,* who had no library experience. During his nine years as director, the St. Paul Public Library lost support and funding. Budgets for book purchasing and staffing suffered. Eventually, the collection began to decline, and as a result, circulation, which had been climbing fast, did not increase. In 1922, the head of the Branch Division reported that her staff compensated for the shrinking budget by creating 100 scrapbooks for very small children from pictures salvaged from discarded children's books which had survived the library fire in 1915.[32] In 1924, Wheelock even proposed closing the branches to free up funds for book purchases.[33]

In frustration, a citizen's group raised money in 1928 to hire Arthur Bostwick and Carl Vitz, two nationally known librarians, to survey the St. Paul Public Library and make recommendations. Their report concluded that the library's biggest need was increased funding for books. They also concluded that St. Paul needed more branch libraries, suggesting that a city of that size should have between eight and ten.[34] In fact, the library was able to open two new branches in spite of its financial problems, the result of a lawsuit which established that the library could finally use proceeds from the estate of Judge Henry Hale who had died in 1890. These funds were used to build the Hamline-Midway branch and the Merriam Park library. For years, there had been a "branch" library in the Hamline area, but it was a small rented space. Community groups in both neighborhoods had long campaigned for new branch buildings and raised money to purchase the sites.[35]

The new branches opened in 1930 before the library began to feel the full impact of the Depression. In 1932, a full-blown financial crisis hit the library. Jennie Jennings, who had become the chief librarian at the death of Webster Wheelock in 1931, wrote an impassioned letter asking library supporters to protest a proposed budget which would require the closing of branch libraries. She also called attention to the fact that salaries had already been cut in 1931 and 1932, and that a further enforced leave without pay was being considered.[36] She was forced to close the main library and all the branches for Thanksgiving weekend 1932. The worst year was 1935 when the entire system was shut down for 15 days in the late summer. Jennings decided that this was better than permanently closing one or more branches.[37]

All five branches survived the Depression but with seriously depleted resources. By 1931, before the Depression began to shrink the number of new books the library could buy, Arlington Hills had about 12,800 books which were loaned about 105,500 times, representing a turnover rate of nearly 8. In those years, Arlington Hills tended to circulate more books than the Riverview or St. Anthony branches.[38] Circulation declined during the 1930s, primarily because there were fewer books to borrow, and declined even further during World War II. By 1945, circulation had shrunk to 50,000, half of what it had been in 1931.

In the midst of this turmoil, the St. Paul Public Library took time to celebrate the fiftieth anniversary of its founding in 1882. The Arlington Hills Library Association hosted an open house in October 1932, which demonstrated that the community continued to value the library. Representatives of four churches spoke briefly to a crowd of about 200, as did a school principal, a business leader, and an officer of the American Legion. Jennie Jennings and the city's commissioner of education also attended. Musical entertainment was once again provided by Johnson High School musicians, along with the Mothers' Singers club of the high school. John Schweitz, the man who led the fundraising to purchase the lots for the library in 1916, also spoke, this time representing the Polish-American Club.[39]

Those celebrating that day could not have known that what they had created on the East Side, including the library, had entered a difficult period. The full impact of the Depression would soon be felt, then the world war would begin, and after the war, great changes would shake the economic foundations of the East Side. The neighborhood's campaign for a library of its own was far from over.

A Closer Look...

Swede Hollow

The Saga of Swede Hollow

by Steve Trimble

Even though it has been gone for half a century, there are people who still remember it fondly. Although some say it was a slum, others think it was a nurturing community that welcomed waves of immigrants to their first home in a new land. It was not large—around eighteen acres—bisected by a creek and tucked into a valley with sixty- to eighty-foot-high cliffs that hid its homes from the outside world.

An 1886 newspaper headline declared it "A Foreign Settlement in the Midst of St. Paul." One winter day, a reporter had taken a look at "the little hamlet of shanties" that was filled with a "flaxen-haired population." According to *The St. Paul Globe,* the area was almost exclusively residential. "There are no stores, a single saloon being the only public place within the valley." It was in "the front room of a little shanty and is kept by a woman."

Swedish immigrants began settling there in the 1860s. According to the 1886 reporter, there were around 110 families in the hollow, and the total population was estimated at around 600. Nels Hokanson, a Swedish man who grew up there, wrote about some of his family's activities: "In the evenings, friends often came to share the warmth, drink coffee, take snuff or smoke their curved Swedish pipes," Nels wrote. "Mother spun wool or knitted and listened to the talk from her place in a corner under a picture of King Oscar II of Sweden." While the area was always ethnically diverse,

Scandinavians predominated in the early years, and the area became known as "Svenska Dalen" or Swede Hollow.

As the Swedes moved "up onto the street," others took their places. In the early 1900s, Italian immigrants moved into Swede Hollow. One of these former residents was Gentille Yarusso, who later wrote about the community. "This enchanted landscape," he remembered, "... resembled the place they had left behind. They loved the hills, the trees, the stream, the security of friends and relatives."

Swede Hollow's kids posed for a photographer around 1935.

Mike Sanchelli, born in Swede Hollow in 1915, was another resident of the neighborhood at the time. His parents owned a house at 22 North Phalen Creek—that's how the addresses ran in a neighborhood with no streets. Looking back on his childhood, he thought it was a "great place to be poor," at least until the Depression, "when it seemed that money had disappeared from the face of the earth." His family had a few chickens, rabbits, and an occasional pig. Eventually, he was able to bring some money home thanks to a Works Progress Administration job.

The boxcar chapel where Mexican-Americans worshipped in Swede Hollow.

Next, Mexicans began joining the Swede Hollow colony, adding their own customs and, as those before them, finding jobs.

Alberta Silva Rodriquez was among the last people to live there. She remembered times of sharing when the Mexican women would trade onions, garlic, and peppers for Italian bread cooked in outdoor ovens. Her mother and an Italian neighbor were able to communicate. "I don't know how," Alberta said, "but they did."

In 1956, the city Health Department decided that since Swede Hollow had no sewer or city water service, it was a health hazard. The last 14 families were moved out and the remaining homes burned down by the Fire Department. Thanks to the efforts of Friends of Swede Hollow and the City of St. Paul, the hollow has been revitalized and is once again a center of the community. In 1973, Swede Hollow was designated a St. Paul Park. The restoration of Swede Hollow was the St. Paul Garden Club's Bicentennial project, for which they received a major award. A section of Phalen Creek, which had been diverted into a large storm sewer, was "daylighted" so it flowed through pools that attracted wildlife. Visitors can now walk or bike through the park on new trails. Still, there are a few reminders of the old days seen in sporadic remains of stone foundations and flowers that were planted in immigrant yards.

Burning the last homes in Swede Hollow in 1956.

Steve Trimble has lived in Dayton's Bluff since the late 1970s. He is a retired college history teacher and has written several books and articles about the Twin Cities. He served part of the East Side in the Minnesota House of Representatives from 1987 to 2000. He has also served on the city's Heritage Preservation Commission and the Editorial Board of the Ramsey County Historical Society.

- Chapter 3 Endnotes -

[1] Brochure entitled "A Souvenir of the Payne Avenue Carnival and Street Fair—Under the Direction of the East Side Commercial Club, 1906" at the Minnesota Historical Society library.

[2] Gwen Westerman and Bruce White, *Mni Sota Makoce: The Land of the Dakota* (St. Paul: Minnesota Historical Society Press, 2012), p. 15, 19.

[3] David A. Lanegran, "Swedish Neighborhoods of the Twin Cities: From Swede Hollow to Arlington Heights, From Snoose Boulevard to Minnehaha Parkway," p. 40–41 in Philip J. Anderson and Dag Blanck, *Swedes in the Twin Cities* (St. Paul: Minnesota Historical society Press, 2001); Greg Brick, *Historic Waters of the Capitol Region Watershed District, Ramsey County, Minnesota* (November 2008), Appendix, D–15–17.

[4] Lanegran, pp 39–56.

[5] Lanegran, p. 46

[6] Carole S. Zellie, "Payne Avenue State Bank," *National Register of Historic Places Nomination Form,* 2007. Available on the web pages of the Minnesota Historical Society or the National Park Service.

[7] Zellie, Section 8, p. 3.

[8] Lanegran, p. 47–48; John W. Diers and Aaron Isaacs, *Twin Cities by Trolley: The Streetcar Era in Minneapolis and St. Paul* (Minneapolis: University of Minnesota Press, 2007), p. 276–277.

[9] Garneth O. Peterson, "The Historic Payne Avenue Business District," a report for the East Side Neighborhood Development Company, St. Paul, 1999.

[10] See Chapter Two

[11] John Sielaff, Biography of Nils Nelson on the "Who Built Our Capitol" Website (www.whobuiltourcapitol.org).

[12] *St. Paul City Directory,* 1915.

[13] Carl Chrislock, *The Progressive Era in Minnesota* (St. Paul: Minnesota Historical Society Press, 1971), p. 120–122.

[14] Carl Chrislock, *Watchdog of Loyalty: the Minnesota Commission of Public Safety During World War I.* (St. Paul: Minnesota Historical Society Press, 1991).

[15] *Legislative Manual of the State of Minnesota 1919* (St, Paul: Secretary of State, 1919), p. 190–191: Chrislock, Watchdog, p. 295–307; Michael J. Lansing, *Insurgent Democracy: The Nonpartisan League in North American Politics* (Chicago: University of Chicago Press, 2015), p. 142–143.

[16] Ann Regan, "The Irish" pp 138, in June Drenning Holmquist, *They Chose Minnesota: A Survey of the State's Ethnic Groups* (St. Paul: Minnesota Historical Society Press, 1981) .

[17] Rudi Vercoli, "The Italians," pp 453–454, 459 in *They Chose Minnesota.* The Christ Child Center was renamed Merrick Community Services in the 1940s. It continues to serve the community at 965 Payne.

[18] *Polish American Club: 59 Years, 1927–1977* (St. Paul: 1977). This 77-page booklet has information about the history of the club. It also has advertisements for Schweitz's Bar at 956 Payne and Schweitz Liquors at 1100 Arcade. The bar at 956 Payne continues today as Brunson's Pub and there is still a liquor store at 1100 Arcade.

[19] Dennis Valdes, *Barrios Nortenos: St. Paul and Midwestern Mexican Communities in the Twentieth Century* (Austin: University of Texas Press, 2000), p. 1122, 135.

[20] "Four Local Libraries to be dedicated soon," *St. Paul Pioneer Press,* September 17, 1917.

[21] Annual Report of the St. Paul Public Library, 1914; Annual Report, 1918. St. Paul Public Library Records, Minnesota Historical Society (147.F.3.1B).

[22] "Registration Report" from the Annual Report of the St. Paul Public Library, 1922. St. Paul Public Library Records, Minnesota Historical Society (147.F.3.1B).

[23] Quoted in Kermit B. Westerberg, "Libraries, Immigrants, Communities," p. 255 in Philip Anderson and Dag Blanck, *Swedes in the Twin Cities* (St. Paul: Minnesota Historical Society Press, 2001).

[24] Westerberg, p. 263–265.

[25] Kathryn Gorman, "Arlington Hills Librarian Retiring," *St. Paul Dispatch,* August 30, 1950.

[26] Arlington Hills Public Library Branch Report for 1945, p. 5. St. Paul Public Library Records, Minnesota Historical Society (147.F.3.3B). This version of the association was apparently short lived, but it would be revived in the future.

[27] Gratia Countryman, "The Library as a Social Centre," 433–437 in Arthur Bostwick, ed. *Classics of American Librarianship: The Library and Society* (New York: Wilson Company, 1920). She argued that the library "should be managed in the broadest spirit of hospitality; the atmosphere should be a gracious, kindly and sympathetic as one own home." (437)

[28] Annual Report of the St. Paul Public Library, 1918, 1919, 1920, 1921, 1922.

[29] "Registration Report" in the Annual Report, 1918, 1922.

[30] "Arlington Branch Library," *The Library Beacon,* Vol 4, No. 8 (December 1932).

[31] Biloine W. Young, *A Noble Task: The Saint Paul Public Library Celebrates 125!* (Afton, MN: Afton Historical Society Press, 2007), p. 78.

[32] "Branch Division Report," Annual Report, 1922.

[33] Young, p. 84.

[34] A. E. Bostwick and Carl Vinz, *Survey of the St. Paul Public Library* (1929)

[35] Young, p 145–147.

[36] Open Letter signed by Mrs. T. B. Jennings, Librarian, no date. In the St. Paul Public Library Records, Minnesota Historical Society 147.F.3.8F).

[37] Gary Phelps, "The St. Paul Public Library and its First 100 Years," 18 *Ramsey County History,* No 1 (1982), p. 17.

[38] Annual Reports, 1917, 1920, 1931.

[39] "Branch Library Fetes Concluded," *St. Paul Pioneer Press,* October 12, 1932.

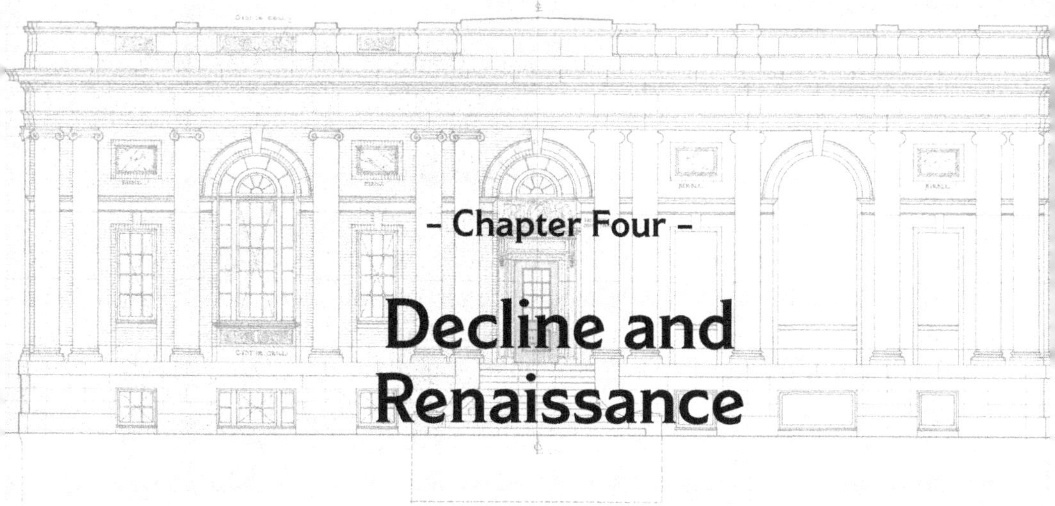

– Chapter Four –

Decline and Renaissance

For a decade or so after World War II, life on the East Side seemed much like it had been before the war. Below the surface, however, great social changes were gaining steam that would transform the area in the 1960s and 1970s. The national wave of deindustrialization began to erode the East Side's economic base. Some 15,000 unionized blue-collar jobs disappeared. Many descendants of the original immigrant families moved to other neighborhoods, sometimes even to other cities. The retail businesses created by Swedish immigrants on Payne Avenue began to close. In the 1980s and 1990s, poverty was increasing, and the outlook of the East Side was bleak. However, new groups of immigrants began to settle in the neighborhood. They came from Asia, like the Hmong from Southeast Asia or the Karen from Myanmar, or from various countries in Latin America, especially Mexico. Soon they would be opening new shops and restaurants on Payne Avenue, part of the renaissance which continues today.

The three Carnegie branches at Arlington Hills, St. Anthony, and Riverview celebrated their 50th birthdays in 1967. Some saw them as part of the historic legacy of their neighborhoods, while others looked on them as aging buildings that had outlived their usefulness. Without a doubt, the city would have to invest in some upgrades if they were to continue to fulfill their function. Like libraries everywhere, they were also dealing with increasing demand, technological change, and new ideas about accessibility. On the East Side, the Arlington Hills library struggled with the challenge of being a resource for the new groups of immigrants. Before these issues could be sorted out, a budget crisis threatened the future of the Arlington Hills branch, provoking a community response.

The Evolving East Side

Through the 1950s, many East Side residents continued to experience Payne Avenue as a kind of small-town main street, not much different than it had been after World War I. Remembering her East Side adolescence, DeAnne Marie Cherry recalled that Sundberg Drug, the original site of the library's transfer station, sponsored her candidacy to be queen of the 1957 Payne Avenue Fall Harvest Festival. She celebrated her 21st birthday at Schweitz Bar, the establishment associated with the family of John L. Schweitz, the man who led the fundraising for the new library.[1]

Looking south down Payne Avenue, decked out for the Harvest Festival in 1952.

Economic and social changes undermined the generations-old businesses of retailers and independent professionals. Some of the children and grandchildren of the original immigrants who had been their customers, moved to other neighborhoods or suburbs as they became more affluent. Others were forced to move as their workplaces closed and they sought new jobs. Meanwhile, family-owned retailers had to compete with large supermarket chains which offered lower prices and more selection. In those same years, the federal government built Interstate Highways 94 and 35E, which made it easy to shop farther from home, including at the new suburban malls.[2] The biggest change, however, was the crumbling of the neighborhood's economic foundations as the East Side's major manufacturing firms succumbed to the processes of consolidation and deindustrialization. At its peak, Seeger Refrigerator had employed 4,000 at its Arcade Street plant. Whirlpool Corporation acquired Seeger in 1955, and by the time it decided to close the plant in 1984, the workforce had shrunk to 625 employees. Hamm's Brewery grew to one of the largest beer companies in the United States, employing 1,300 workers in the 1950s. The family sold it in 1965, and after it changed hands a number of times, what was left of its production capacity was shut down in 1997.[3] The 3M plant at Arcade and East Seventh had employed 4,300. In the late 1950s, 3M bought a big plot of land in Maplewood and slowly began moving its manufacturing to its growing campus there. 3M had shrunk its East Side workforce to 1,500 employees by 2000 and finally shut the plant down in 2008.[4] This massive loss of well-paid union jobs was devastating to the neighborhood. As a result, the small business and shops which had prospered along Payne Avenue for decades mostly didn't survive the 1960s.

Into this deindustrialized landscape moved new waves of immigrants. Many Hmong people, who had migrated into Southeast Asia from southern China in the early 1800s, were caught up in the tragic American interventions in Southeast Asia following the French defeat by Vietnamese nationalists in 1954. To support the American war effort in neighboring Vietnam, the Central Intelligence Agency recruited Hmong military leader Vang Pao to organize a Hmong guerilla army to wage a secret war in Laos. Of the 30,000 Hmong soldiers who fought between 1961 and 1975, over 17,000 were killed, along with many civilians. After the United States defeat, many more Hmong were killed trying to escape to Thailand.[5]

In 1976, Congress facilitated the resettlement of Hmong refugees in the United States, and remarkably, Minnesota became one of the major destinations. By 2000, about 42,000 Hmong had come to Minnesota, particularly to St. Paul's East Side. As the Hmong community became more established, its members organized large

Mee Moua represented the East Side in the Minnesota Senate from 2002 to 2011.

sports festivals and New Year's celebrations. The Twin Cities was sometimes referred to as the "Hmong capital of the world."[6] The Hmong migration from the Laotian highlands to St. Paul was difficult, but after about 40 years, many Hmong have sunk deep roots in Minnesota. Mee Moua, who was born in war-torn Laos, became the first Hmong American elected to a state legislature when she became the senator representing the East Side in 2002. She left the Senate in 2011, and today Senator Foung Hawj, another Hmong immigrant born in Laos, represents the East Side. He is part of a contingent of five Hmong Americans in the Minnesota Legislature. Dai Thao, another Hmong American, sits on the St. Paul City Council.

Mexicans had come to the East Side beginning in the early 1920s, and they continued to live in Swede Hollow after World War II. However, the city never provided water and sewer service to the area, and in 1956, the city condemned the area and burnt down the remaining houses. In the 1970s, the ravine was turned into a park. Many of the early Mexican residents had, by this time, gone "up the hill" to other neighborhoods in the East End, and they were soon joined by a new wave of Mexicans, along with immigrants from other countries in Latin America, especially El Salvador. In 2008, the city acknowledged this community by dedicating Aguirre Avenue on the East Side, honoring the ten sons of an East Side Mexican-American family who served in the United States military from World War II to Vietnam. They were among the fifteen children of Joseph and Henrietta Aguirre, who had moved to the East Side in the 1920s.[7]

Like their European predecessors, new immigrants sought the food and clothing with which they had grown up. As older businesses closed on Payne Avenue, immigrants created new businesses similar to the early Swedish, Italian, and German shops. There are Asian groceries and various *supermercados,* including La Palma which is Salvadoran and Bymore which is Mexican. The Plaza Latina provides a home to a restaurant and a number of shops. There are also various *taquerias* and other places featuring Mexican and Central American food; and restaurants serving Asian foods, including East Side Thai, a Hmong-owned restaurant managed by the children of the family that opened it many years ago, and Cook St. Paul, which features Korean-inspired food.

Plaza Latina, a Payne Avenue *mercado* with a restaurant and other businesses.

While new immigrants have been moving in, the descendants of some pre-World War I immigrants continue to live in the East Side and carry on their cultural traditions. The Railroad Island neighborhood, for example, features Yarusso Brothers Restaurant and Morelli's Alimentary, two legacies of the Italian immigration to the East Side around 1900. From this community emerged Bruce Vento, who grew up on the East Side a few blocks north of Railroad Island. His father was an officer in the Machinists' Union. He went to Johnson High School and eventually became a science teacher in the Minneapolis public schools. In 1970, he was elected to the first of three terms in the Minnesota House, and in 1976, he was elected to represent St. Paul in the U.S. Congress. He became nationally known as a protector of the environment and a champion of the National Parks. He was also respected for his advocacy for the homeless. When the Hmong began to settle in St. Paul, he sponsored legislation to support them and make the path to citizenship easier. He died in 2000 at age 60, during his 12th term in Congress. He died of lung cancer, the result of the asbestos to which he was exposed while working in several factory jobs when he was younger.[8] Shortly before he died, the public school a block from his boyhood home was renamed the Bruce Vento Elementary School. The city has also created the Bruce Vento Nature Sanctuary in the area where Turner and Phalen creeks once entered the Mississippi.

Bruce Vento, the East Side's congressman, served in the U.S. House from 1977 until his death in 2000.

The Library in Changing Times

The public library had to deal with these social and economic changes, especially in the city's neighborhoods. Perrie Jones, who had been appointed head librarian in 1936, was dedicated to extending library services beyond the traditional downtown library. Under her leadership, the St. Paul Public Library recovered economically after World War II and resumed the process of expanding into the neighborhoods. The library got its first real bookmobile in 1949 and went on to build three new branches in the early 1950s. These were financed in part by the sale of the Market House property which had technically been owned by the library since 1899. A lawsuit established that the proceeds should benefit the library and not the general fund of the city.[9] The city built the Rice Street branch in 1952, the Highland Park branch in 1954, and the Hayden Heights branch in 1955.

The building of branches continued under J. Archer Eggen, who became the library director in 1955. After a long controversy about the location of the next branch, the city bought an old theater on University Avenue near Lexington Parkway and transformed it in 1967 into the Lexington branch. At the time, it was the city's largest branch and the only one with air conditioning. In 1970, the city added the Sun Ray branch, named for a shopping center near the city's eastern border. The five libraries built after World War II brought the total number of branches in St. Paul to ten. Some of these modernist buildings would have short lifespans. The Highland Park branch, however, was remodeled and enlarged in 1975.

Under Eggen, the city also decided to "modernize" the three Carnegie libraries—from new roofs and upgraded boiler systems to interior makeovers that included suspended ceilings of acoustical tiles with egg-crate fluorescent lights, vinyl asbestos flooring, Venetian blinds, and spruce green paint on the walls.[10] The circulation desks, originally across from the main entrance vestibule, were replaced by new desks just to the south of the main entrance. The libraries also received all new furniture, including metal library tables with green Formica tops, lounge chairs with striped cushions, and a "flop bench" for children, with bittersweet orange upholstery. The Payne Avenue Business Association and the local Boy Scout troop sponsored the April 1958 open house at the Arlington Hills branch which gave visitors an opportunity to admire the new "modern" look of their Carnegie library.[11]

It took a while to recover from the years of the Great Depression and World War II, but the St. Paul Public Library eventually began to expand the number of people it served. In 1956, the year Perrie Jones retired, nearly 90,000 citizens held library cards, the most ever, and they borrowed books, periodicals, or phonograph records about 1.5 million times, approaching the circulation figures achieved before the war. Jones bolstered support for the library by organizing the Friends of the St. Paul Public Library in 1945. This organization lent its support in a quiet, behind-the-scenes way for many years. That changed in 1972 when it received a $1.6 million bequest from the

Children try out the "flop bench" added to the children's department in the 1958 remodeling.

John and Myrtle Briggs estate, the first of several major gifts. Now in control of a major endowment, the Friends have been a significant force in library development since then.[12]

With the support of the Friends, the library was actively involved in community outreach in the 1960s and 1970s. The library owned a van which took puppet shows and story hours to the neighborhoods. The library even had its own radio show. This was, as the historian of the St. Paul Public Library wrote, the "golden age of library programming."[13] However, by the late 1970s, funding for these activities began to disappear, and eventually, the office that organized these events was closed and the van sold.

The situation at the Arlington Hills branch was similar. Circulation was growing primarily because the librarians worked hard to connect with local schools and provide story hours and a children's summer reading program. Although children were their priority, one annual report by the branch librarian mentioned that men from Seeger Refrigerator used the library to research technical issues and that others came to study for civil service exams.[14] By 1958, the year that the remodeling was completed, the branch loaned books, periodicals, and records over 78,000 times, the highest number since the 1930s. Circulation continued to grow and peaked at 114,595 in 1968. Like their colleagues across the system, the Arlington Hills librarians focused on outreach, maintaining active relationships not only with the schools but with community organizations like Merrick Community Services. The children's program of the library even had a contingent in the annual Harvest Festival Parade on Payne Avenue.[15]

In 1969, however, circulation at the branch began a slow decline. In an annual report, the librarian attributed this to the fact that Arlington Hills, which had always been closed on Sundays, now lost its Saturday hours as well. For example, in the summer of 1973, the branch was only open 41 hours per week (from 12:30 to 9 on Monday and Tuesday, and 9:30 to 5:30 on Wednesday, Thursday, and Friday). This could not help but reduce the number of books circulated. Back in 1957, the branch librarian told the newspaper that "our typical patron" was a housewife whose husband worked at 3M or Hamm's Brewery. "As soon as her children can print their names," she brings them to get a library card.[16] By the 1970s, those manufacturing jobs were disappearing, and children were increasingly being raised in families where all the adults had jobs. If the library was closed all weekend, it followed that working families would visit the library less and borrow fewer books.

From Crisis to National Recognition

The St. Paul Public Library had survived the Great Depression without closing a branch. By the early 1970s, however, public libraries were squeezed between the growing demand for their services on the one hand, and a decreasing level of funding for libraries on the other. Not only were the wealthy less likely to make large gifts to public institutions, but the country was experiencing a series of recessions, major ones in 1973–1975 and 1980–1982, and a briefer one in 1990–1991, which led to shrinking library budgets. Not surprisingly, when city officials sought to cut spending, the library system seemed to be an easy place to start. Librarians often found it difficult to restore pre-recession funding levels once the economy had begun to rebound. This erosion of support happened with little public notice because people tend to take their library for granted until a crisis threatens its survival. "While libraries have few outright enemies," one astute observer remarked, "they have lots of lukewarm friends."[17] In the world's wealthiest country, the drastic cuts which were avoided during the Great Depression were suddenly on the table. The very future of the Arlington Hills, Riverview, and Hamline branches was being called into question.

In 1978, the Minnesota League of Women Voters issued a report calling attention to the underfunding of libraries statewide. The report noted that library systems were increasingly cutting services and hours, replacing paid staff with volunteers, and even charging fees.[18] St. Paul was no exception and budgets declined throughout the 1970s.[19] When Gerald Steenberg took over as director of the St. Paul Public Library in 1978, he was forced to further reduce the number of hours libraries were open, cut back on staff, and shrink budgets for new materials. The library seemed to be in a downward spiral. Looking for solutions, Mayor George Latimer appointed a Citizen's Task Force in 1979 to prepare a five-year plan for the St. Paul Public Library. Humphrey Doermann, the president of the Bush Foundation, chaired the task force, which hired a Texas consulting firm to prepare a report with recommendations. The process was funded by the St. Paul Foundation, the Friends of the Library, and the Perrie Jones Fund, the result of a half a million-dollar bequest by the former head librarian who had died in 1968. The consultants submitted their report in February 1981, and based on that report, the task force issued its final recommendations to the mayor and city council on May 1, 1981.

George Latimer during his tenure as mayor of St. Paul.

The consultants were of the opinion that St. Paul could not afford ten full-service branch libraries. They recommended dividing the branches into five full-service "area community libraries" and five "neighborhood community libraries" that offered reduced services and limited hours. Arlington Hills, Riverview, Merriam Park, Hamline, and Rice Street libraries were put in the second category, because they were the "smaller and less effective libraries," according to the consultants. In its final report, the Task Force went further, recommending that the Arlington Hills and Riverview libraries be closed and that their services be moved to "more modest locations," such as a community center. The task force also recommended that the city take "a close look" at treating the Hamline Library the same way.[20]

In fact, J. Archer Eggen had quietly sought funding six years earlier to replace the Carnegie-funded Arlington Hills branch with a new building at Payne Avenue and Rose Street. In an unsuccessful Community Development Block Grant application in 1975, he argued that the community needed a new one-story building with off-street parking. Such a building, he wrote, would provide a larger, more flexible space and avoid the problems caused by the exterior and interior stairways.[21] During those years, the building and maintenance supervisor of the St. Paul Public Library recommended closing the Arlington Hills Public Library not only because it was not handicapped accessible, but also because it needed new windows, doors, stair and sidewalk repairs, and upgraded plumbing and wiring.[22] Roofs must be regularly replaced, and buildings from the World War I era eventually need electrical and plumbing improvements. The windows, however, would not have deteriorated if they had been properly maintained. The fire marshal had also restricted occupancy of the basement auditoriums of the three Carnegie branches because of limited exits. All of these problems were correctable, but for many people, building new always makes more sense than renovation.

In any case, the moment of crisis had finally come for citizens who used these three branches. In all three neighborhoods, groups came together to save their library. Eastsiders went to a July 15 public meeting at the Arlington Hills Public Library and heard Gerald Steenberg explain that he had been instructed to cut 10 percent out of the library budget and that the task force had recommended closing libraries with the lowest level of use. Councilwoman Joanne Showalter was also present and told people to write the mayor and council members and to expect that budgets would continue to get tighter in coming years. Some in attendance decided to form an organization to support the Arlington Hills Library, and in a few months the Arlington Hills Library Association was born—a group which worked to save the branch and then continued to support it for many years.[23]

Meanwhile, a turning point was reached on the West Side, where over 600 people came to a July 29 open meeting to express their passionate support for the Riverview branch to Mayor George Latimer and Gerald Steenberg. Following the meeting, the mayor announced that closing any of the three branches was off the table.[24] Unfortunately, this did not solve the lack of funding, and for the next several years the branches suffered through staff cuts, drastic decreases in children's programming, and shortened hours. The hours at the Arlington Hills branch were cut to 37 per week in 1982, and all children's and adult programming was ended.[25] That year, yet another task force recommended balancing the budget by closing Arlington Hills, arguing that its circulation did not justify the cost of keeping it open.[26]

The Arlington Hills Library Association successfully lobbied to keep their branch open, and they also encouraged greater public use of the branch. Circulation, which had reached 114,000 annually in the late 1960s, had fallen to under 70,000. The association worked hard to raise the profile of the branch by organizing forums, fundraisers, and contests, and by publishing a regular column in the *Eastsider* newspaper.[27] By the end of 1982, circulation began to pick up, and it continued to grow each year, reaching nearly 85,000 by 1985.

While these events were unfolding, the three Carnegie branches, which had celebrated their 50th birthdays in 1967, began to be seen as historic buildings worthy of preservation. Congress had passed the National Historic Preservation Act in 1966 which set up, among other things, the National Register of Historic Places. This federal program highlights buildings worthy of preservation and celebrates them, but does not protect them from demolition or alteration. Between 1980 and 1982, the Ramsey County Historical Society and the City of St. Paul's Heritage Preservation Commission sponsored a massive survey of over 5,000 buildings in the county. The survey team concluded that the Arlington Hills, St. Anthony Park, and Riverview branches were eligible for the National Register because they were significant historically for their association with Andrew Carnegie's library philanthropy and also significant architecturally as outstanding examples of the Beaux Arts tradition in St. Paul.[28]

Based on this review, the State Historic Preservation Office facilitated the nomination of the three Carnegie branches to the National Register, a process that was formally completed in 1984.[29] The following year, the city's Heritage Preservation Commission designated the three branch libraries as local historic landmarks. Unlike the National Register, the designation under a local heritage preservation ordinance does offer some protection to the historic property. A property owner must obtain the approval of the HPC before demolishing or significantly altering the building.

Back from the Brink

Thanks to grassroots neighborhood action, the libraries that had earlier been threatened with demolition were now scheduled for improvements. The renovation included all three Carnegie libraries, mostly financed through the city's capital improvement budget.[30] At Arlington Hills, the exterior masonry was repointed in 1985, a new roof was installed in 1986, and in 1988, the original wood windows were replaced by aluminum-framed windows which looked much like the originals. Meanwhile, a basement window opening on the west façade was converted into a new exterior entrance to the auditorium which satisfied the Fire Marshall's concern about the limited exits in the basement. All plumbing pipes and electrical wiring were replaced, and a new central heating, ventilating and air conditioning system was installed. Finally, the circulation desk was returned to its original position across from the main entrance, and the main reading room got new carpets. In this last stage, the exterior stairs leading from the sidewalk to the main entrance were repaired and new handrails installed.[31]

Kao Kalia Yang

By the 1990s, the growing numbers of Hmong settling in St. Paul and the East Side led the librarians to adjust their outreach approaches and search for ways to build their collection of adult and children's books in Hmong. Arlington Hills was one of the branches which specialized in English as Second Language materials. Kao Kalia Yang, who was born in a Hmong refugee camp in Thailand and became a writer and teacher, recalled how her father brought her to the Arlington Hills branch to borrow books. She found a step stool so that she could reach books for herself, having as a child "no voice in English to ask for help." Now she is an established author, having published two award-winning memoirs about Hmong migration and life.[32]

The St. Paul system continued to grow, loaning items about 2.6 million times in 1991. St. Paul's population was then about 272,000, which meant that there were 9.7 loans per resident, one of the highest ratios in the country. At the same time, the circulation at the renovated Arlington Hills branch continued to rebound, reaching 110,000 in 1992, the year the three Carnegie libraries celebrated their 75th birthdays. This was largely the result of the fact that, after the lean budget years, the branch had renewed its children's programming with a Young Readers Program and a new, reinvigorated series of story hours. Their work was augmented by a system-wide summer reading program which brought magicians, jugglers, musicians, and others to each branch to attract children to the library. By 1999, the library also had five public internet workstations which were especially popular with children.[33] In their annual reports, librarians credited the Arlington Hills Library Association for continued community support.

The 1997 elevator addition with street level entrance facing Jessamine Street.

The Arlington Hills branch, along with its two Carnegie siblings, needed one more major upgrade. In 1990, Congress passed the Americans with Disabilities Act which required that public buildings be accessible. Minnesota law provided some protection for the disabled even earlier. Most Carnegie libraries—and the three St. Paul branches were no exception—had main floors that were five to six feet above the sidewalk level and reached by stairways inaccessible to a patron who was, for example, in a wheelchair. To solve this problem, the Arlington Hills Library was closed during part of 1997 while a brick elevator addition was added in the rear of the building. The elevator provided access to a new sidewalk level entrance on Jessamine Street. A new ramp was also built to allow access to the auditorium from the interior hallway. At the same time, the suspended ceiling, added in the 1950s, was removed, exposing the historic plasterwork, a new restroom was added, and a brick library sign was constructed at the northeast corner of the property.[34] The Arlington Hills Library Association hosted a grand reopening celebration in December of 1997. The Riverview and St. Anthony branches were also made accessible with elevators. Plus, the St. Anthony branch gained a large circular addition behind the original building to house its children's department.[35]

In 2000, the 83-year-old Carnegie branches entered the 21st Century renovated, energy-efficient, handicapped accessible, and structurally sound. They had in fact, outlived by far, some of the St. Paul branches which had been built later. The Merriam Park branch, built in 1930, starting sinking in the 1970s and had to be replaced with a new building in 1993. The Rice Street branch, built in 1952, lasted only fifty years. A new building opened in 2002. The Hayden Heights Library had an even shorter lifespan. Built in 1955, it was replaced by a new building in 1979. The Sun Ray branch, built in 1970, had a leaky roof and by 2000 had been remodeled twice.[36] In 2014, it was expanded again to accommodate some of the Materials Management Department of the library system.[37]

Meanwhile, the St. Paul Public Library was experimenting with new ways to deliver library services. In 1984, the West Seventh Branch was opened as a small "popular library" offering mostly recreational reading materials. In 1995, the Highland Park branch had been joined with a park district recreation center to form the Highland Park Community Center. This facility was expanded again in 2014. In 2005, the St. Paul Public Library joined with Metropolitan State University to create the twelfth branch, Dayton's Bluff Library, in a building shared with the university's academic library. In 2001, the Lexington Branch was closed for six months after a heavy rain caused flooding which damaged thousands of books. This started a process that led to the replacement of the Lexington branch by the Rondo Community Outreach Library in a new five-story building at University Avenue and Dale Street. Funded by a public-private partnership, the building includes over a hundred residences and underground parking, in addition to the library and other service organizations. The St. Paul Library's bookmobile also finds a home there.[38]

The Arlington Hills, St. Anthony Park, and Riverview branches were doing well. Their communities were enjoying the recent upgrades to each building. The Arlington Hills library circulated items over 92,000 times in 2007, and perhaps more importantly, had about 150,000 patron visits, even though it was open only about 51 hours per week. Its ten computer work stations were well used.[39] Nevertheless, its days were numbered.

A Closer Look...

Reaching Out to the Community

To publicize the Summer Reading Program in 1999, the St. Paul Public Library created bookmarks in English, Spanish, and Hmong.

- Chapter 4 Endnotes -

[1] DeAnne Marie Cherry, "Growing Up in St. Paul: A Stroll Down Memory Lane: Payne Avenue in the 1950s," *Ramsey County History,* Vol, 38, No 3 (Fall 2003): 22–25. These two establishments are mentioned in Chapter Three.

[2] David A. Lanegran, "Swedish Neighborhoods of the Twin Cities: From Swede Hollow to Arlington Heights, From Snoose Boulevard to Minnehaha Parkway," p. 48–49 in Philip J. Anderson and Dag Blanck, *Swedes in the Twin Cities* (St. Paul: Minnesota Historical Society Press, 2001).

[3] Steve Trimble, "From the Land of Sky Blue Waters," *Saint Paul Historical,* accessed September 25, 2017, http://saintpaulhistorical.com/items/show/1.

[4] Nick Woltman, "What Was St. Paul's East Side like in its economic glory days?" *St. Paul Pioneer Press,* August 23, 2016.

[5] Chia Youyee Vang, *Hmong in Minnesota* (St. Paul: Minnesota Historical Society Press, 2008), p. 1–23.

[6] Chia Youyee Vang, *Hmong America: Reconstructing Community in Diaspora* (Urbana: University of Illinois Press, 2010), p. 58–59.

[7] Don Boxmeyer, "St. Paul names road to honor a family," *St. Paul Pioneer Press,* April 20, 2008.

[8] Greg Gordon and Tom Berg, "A Champion until the end," *Minneapolis Star Tribune,* October 11, 2000, p. A1, A20.

[9] Biloine W. Young, *A Noble Task: The Saint Paul Public Library Celebrates 125!* (Afton, MN: Afton Historical Society Press, 2007), p. 56, 85, 116. The St. Paul Public Library occupied the second floor of the Market House at 7th and Wabasha in downtown from 1900 until the building burnt down in 1915. See Chapter One.

[10] This had the effect of lowering by four feet the 18-foot ceiling for which Charles Hausler had campaigned so strenuously in 1916. See Chapter Two.

[11] "3 Libraries Display 'New Look' Thursday," *St. Paul Pioneer Press,* April 19, 1958; "Remodeled Library Encourages Readers," *St. Paul Pioneer Press,* December 4, 1958: "The New Look," leaflet advertising the open house on April 28, 1958 (from archives of the Arlington Hills Public Library).

[12] Young, p. 157–158.

[13] Young, p. 129.

[14] Agnes Kerr, "Arlington Branch Library Annual Report for 1950." This and other branch reports at the Arlington Hills Public Library archive.

[15] "Annual Report of Arlington Hills – 1958"; Elizabeth McMonigal, "Arlington Hills Branch Library Annual Report – 1969."

[16] Elizabeth McMonigal, "Arlington Hills Branch Library Annual Report – 1969"; Lois Pearson, "Arlington Hills Branch Library," PACC News, August 1973; "Libraries Note Varied Book Taste," *St. Paul Pioneer Press,* May 26, 1957.

[17] Quoted in League of Women Voters in Minnesota, "Funding of Public Libraries in Minnesota," November 1978, p 8. The speaker was Major Owen, a librarian who represented Brooklyn in the United States House of Representatives for 24 years. The quote is from his speech to the 1973 convention of the Minnesota Library Association.

[18] League of Women Voters in Minnesota, "Funding of Public Libraries in Minnesota," November 1978, p. 8–9.

[19] Young, p. 152

[20] HBW Associates, *An Era of Anticipation: Saint Paul Public Library, Service Response to Change,* February 1981; Citizens Task Force for the Library, *Report to the Mayor and the City Council of the City of St. Paul,* May 1, 1981.

[21] J. Archer Eggen, "Community Development Block Grant Program—Project Scope of Services Form, October 14, 1975." The proposal called for a 6,000 square foot building. The Carnegie branch had about 3,600 sq. ft. on each of its two levels. This document, which may be a draft, is in the archives of the Arlington Hills Public Library, Box 1, Folder 5.

[22] St. Paul Public Library Annual Report, 1980. St. Paul Public Library Records, Minnesota Historical Society (147.F.3.6F).

[23] "Community Support Growing for Arlington Hills Library," *The Eastsider,* August, 1981, p. 13; "Arlington Hills Library Committee Forming," *The Eastsider,* September 1981, p. 23; "Arlington Hills Branch Committee Off to a Good Start," *The Eastsider,* October 1981, p. 15; "Arlington Hills Library Association Formed," *The Eastsider,* December 1981, p. 25.

[24] Don Ahern, "Mayor hears pleas to retain library," *St. Paul Dispatch,* July 29, 1981, p. 1C; Dane Smith, "Mayor seeks plan to save 3 libraries," *St. Paul Pioneer Press,* July 30, 1981, p. 1.

[25] "Reduce Hours of Service for Arlington Hills Branch Library," *The Eastsider,* January 1982, p. 23.

[26] "The Planning Council News," *The Eastsider,* August 1982, p. 25. Circulation statistics are related to hours of service. Reduced hours usually result in reduced circulation.

[27] These articles were written by Denise Carlson and appeared in the issues of *The Eastsider* beginning in August 1982 (p. 25) and ran into 1983.

[28] "The Planning Council News," *The Eastsider,* February 1984, p. 14. Susan Roth of the State Historic Preservation Office appeared before the District 5 Planning Council in January 1984 to update the council on the process of adding the library to the National Register.

[29] Patricia Murphy et. al. "St. Anthony Park, Arlington Hills, and Riverview Carnegie Libraries." *National Register of Historic Places Inventory-Nomination Form,* November 12, 1981. This form was initially prepared as part of a survey of historic sites of St. Paul and Ramsey County. The three buildings were not formally "listed" on the National Register until February 4, 1984.

[30] Don Ahern, "Neighbors rally to get library improvements," *St. Paul Pioneer Press,* December 1988.

[31] Karen E. Smith, 1988 Annual Report-Arlington Hills Branch Library. Archives of the Arlington Hills Public Library.

[32] Kao Kalia Yang, "Invisible Stories," pp 111–117 in Doug Ohman, *Libraries of Minnesota* (St. Paul: Minnesota Historical Society, 2011).

[33] Karen Kolb, "Arlington Hills Branch Library 1999 Annual Report." Archives of the Arlington Hills Public Library.

[34] Wiss, Janney, Elstsner Associates, Inc., "East Side Freedom Library Historic Structures Report," May 29, 1915. Suspended ceilings at St. Anthony Park and Riverview had been removed in the 1980s.

[35] Young, p. 143–145.

[36] Young, p. 146–149.

[37] Scott Takushi, "Check Out These Libraries," *St. Paul Pioneer Press,* November 16, 2014, p. B1.

[38] Young, p. 149–150, 195–200.

[39] St. Paul Public Library Facilities Plan, Progress Report, June 2008, p. 3–4

- Chapter Five -

The Library Reinvented Again

The historic Carnegie library on Greenbrier Street has led a charmed existence. Administrators at the St. Paul Public Library talked about closing the library in 1924, 1936, 1975, and 1981. Generally, the closing of this or another branch was linked to anxiety about funding. If budgets were shrinking, maybe something had to go. After library users rallied to save the Arlington Hills and Riverview branches in 1981, the city decided to invest in the Carnegie branches, and in 1997, even added elevators to achieve compliance with the Americans with Disabilities Act. A decade later, however, the St. Paul Public Library teamed with the Parks and Recreation Department to build a community center on Payne Avenue which included a new Arlington Hills Public Library. In 2014, the stately building that Charles Hausler had built on the East Side with Andrew Carnegie's money would be reinvented and find a new life—and a new community connection—as the East Side Freedom Library.

The Last Hurrah

Eastsiders learned that the St. Paul Public Library wanted to replace the Arlington Hills branch in 2007 when library director Melanie Huggins announced the results of a new consultants' report. The report recommended upgrades to the downtown library and most of the branches, but not Arlington Hills, which, the report concluded, did not provide "a comfortable place for adults" because its reading room was dominated by young patrons. Instead, it proposed a new East Side Library which would be a joint facility built with the city's Parks and Recreation Department. Based on this, Huggins said the city would build a new $13 million East Side library to replace the Carnegie building on Greenbrier. Huggins made clear that a new Arlington Hills library was her top priority, and Peter Pearson, president of the Friends of the St. Paul Public Library, agreed that this was a pressing need.[1]

About that same time, Dan Bostrom, a life-long Eastsider who had represented the area on the city council since 1996, helped organize a public-private partnership which aimed to build "a campus of buildings" on a two-block area bounded by Payne, Maryland, Jessamine, and Greenbrier. The project envisioned a new Arlington Hills library under the same roof with a new recreation center, along with various non-governmental occupants.[2] The city's aging recreation center on Rose Street (one block south of Maryland) would be razed and Rose Street vacated between Payne and Greenbrier. The partnership included representatives of the St. Paul Public Library, Parks and Recreation Department, Arlington Hills Lutheran Church, Bradshaw Funeral and Cremation Services, and Merrick Community Services, all of which hoped to find a home in the new project. Shortly thereafter, however, the Great Recession hit and the city was forced to table any discussion of major capital improvements.

Dan Bostrom represented the East Side on the St. Paul City Council from 1995 to 2018.

In 2010, Bostrom learned that Ramsey County wanted to widen the intersection at Payne and Maryland to allow for left turn lanes.[3] This would require the demolition of the 1921 building on the southeast corner that had been home to Kendall's Ace Hardware for about 50 years. Bostrom facilitated the hardware store's sale of the property to the city and its construction of a new building at the corner of Payne and Phalen.[4] The public-private partnership then amended its plan to include a "town square" building at the Payne/Maryland intersection. Bostrom continued to be a strong advocate for the proposal, the first stage of which would be a new building that would contain the library, fitness center, and event space. In a second stage, he envisioned a social service center, a funeral home, a spirituality center, and an "end of life" counseling center, all paid for by private funds. At this point, Merrick Community Services decided to deal with its space needs independently and dropped out of the partnership.[5]

The revised plans were presented at a community forum in August 2011, attended by about 150 Eastsiders. Although many were pleased with the ambitious plans, some felt strongly about retaining their historic Carnegie library, some didn't care much for the design of the new building, and others didn't see why religious institutions should be part of a public building project.[6] After this meeting, the architects revised the plans, and by February 2012, the city was committed to going ahead with the first phase.[7] In August, the city razed the existing recreational center on Rose Street and began work on the new building.

Meanwhile, the city pondered the future of the Carnegie branch on Greenbrier Street. Local residents had consistently made clear that they wanted the building to be restored and reused in a way that would serve the community. The Payne-Phalen District Five Planning Council sent a letter to Kit Hadley, who had taken over as library director in 2009, expressing this desire. Hadley echoed these concerns when she advised the city council that "it is important that the purchaser of this historic structure continue to use it in a manner beneficial to the surrounding community."[8]

The city ordered an appraisal of the Carnegie library and put it up for sale on condition that potential buyers demonstrate a viable business plan based on a reuse of the building that would serve the surrounding community, reflect its history, and enrich the cultural diversity of the area. The city reminded potential buyers that the building was not only on the National Register of Historic Places, but more importantly, had been designated a local landmark by the St. Paul Heritage Preservation Commission. As a result, a potential buyer would need the approval of the city's Heritage Preservation Commission before making any changes to the building, especially on the exterior. The appraised value was $365,000, and under city ordinances, the price was not negotiable.[9]

The Arlington Hills Public Library, and the community which it served, now faced a dangerous moment. Vacant buildings almost unavoidably deteriorate, and this process eventually results in either a depressing eyesore or a demolition permit. Owners of a historic property must find a new function for the building if it will no longer be used for its original purpose. It is essential that the reuse plan be economically sustainable over the long run. This can sometimes be difficult to achieve.

Although Carnegie libraries were very well built and generally have no structural problems, communities have not always found sustainable ways to reuse them. About a third of the 1,679 Carnegie libraries built in the United States had already been razed or repurposed by the early 1990s, and the number is likely higher today. Andrew Carnegie donated funds for 65 public libraries in Minnesota, and today only 22 of them still fulfill their initial purpose. Another 17 have been torn down after they were replaced with a new building and one was lost to fire. Many of the lost buildings fell during the "urban renewal" era of the 1970s. The remaining 25 are being used in a new way: 11 provide office and retail space; six have been converted into art centers by cities or non-profits; two serve as governmental offices; and the remainder offer a mix of uses including a senior center and a historical society's museum. Unlike many former school buildings, no Carnegie library has been converted to residences in Minnesota. Of the 47 surviving buildings, 37 have been listed on the National Register of Historic Places.[10]

The nine branch libraries built by Carnegie in Minnesota cities have survived at a higher rate than their rural cousins. Three of the four Minneapolis branches funded by Carnegie are still used as public libraries. Only the Central Avenue branch built in 1912 has been demolished. The other three—Hosmer, Franklin, and Sumner—all survive thanks to significant additions. In St. Paul, the Carnegie-funded Riverview and St. Anthony Park branches continue to serve their communities. Elevators were installed in both buildings in the 1990s, and the St. Anthony Park library gained a major addition to house its children's department in 1998. On the other hand, the Duluth Public Library abandoned both of its Carnegie-funded branches. One has been demolished and the other sold to a non-profit which converted it into an art school and gallery.

No one advocated demolishing the Arlington Hills branch. However, if the city was not interested in using the building in some new way—and it was not—the range of possible buyers would likely be narrow, especially given its location on a residential street. After the city council approved the sale of the building in March 2013, the Department of Planning and Economic Development asked for proposals by October 30, 2013.[11]

A New Kind of Library for the People

While this process was unfolding, something happened on the East Side that would rescue the building and lead to a new, but closely-related second life. Sometime around 2010, Beth Cleary and Peter Rachleff, two professors at Macalester College in St. Paul, began searching for a way to create a project which would allow them to use their combined skills to contribute to the renaissance of the East Side. In particular, they wanted to build bridges between communities, from the long-standing Native-American, African-American, Mexican-American, and European-American residents of the East Side to the new immigrants from Southeast Asia, Central America, and East Africa. At the time, Rachleff was a member of

Peter Rachleff and Beth Cleary

the History Department, specializing in American labor, African-American, and immigration history, and also a community faculty member at Metropolitan State University. He had studied and written about labor struggles in Minnesota, from strikes on the Iron Range to the meatpackers strike in Austin. Today, Cleary teaches in the Theater and Dance Department, where she had long served as the department chair. She has a strong interest in telling the stories of diverse communities through theatre performance. They have lived in the Dayton's Bluff neighborhood, just a few blocks from Swede Hollow, since 1998.

They found inspiration for their project in New York. In 1998, they met Camille Billops and James V. Hatch, a remarkable couple who had been collecting materials on African-American cultural arts since 1972. Billops is a filmmaker and artist, and Hatch, a theater historian who published some of the first anthologies of African-American playwrights. The couple collected play scripts and theater programs, and also conducted and archived more than 1,500 audio and video interviews of artists. They began the archive in their Lower Manhattan living space, which also functioned as a meeting place for artists. In 2002, they donated a significant portion of their collection to Emory University to make it more available to the public.

James V. Hatch and Camille Billops

Cleary and Rachleff presented Billops' films at Macalester and brought the couple to the college to conduct workshops on racism. They also began collecting materials on the arts, and with the Hatch-Billops archives as a model, envisioned a space which could be both a repository of books and artifacts, and a place where Eastsiders from many backgrounds could share their stories and build bridges between their communities. With the Hatch-Billops example in mind, they developed the idea which would reinvent the Arlington Hills Public Library as the East Side Freedom Library (ESFL).

Assisted by Edward Kodet, one of the Twin Cities leading architects, they began looking at available properties on the East Side. Their searches led to nothing until Tim Mahoney, who represents part of the East Side in the Minnesota House of Representatives, alerted Rachleff and Cleary in 2013 to the fact that the Carnegie library at Arlington Hills was available. Then things kicked into high gear. Rachleff and Cleary created a 501(c)(3) non-profit organization with a board of directors led by Thomas O'Connell, a recently retired professor from Metropolitan State University. Other collaborators included historian Mary Wingerd, the Hmong writer Kao Kalia Yang, and Latino labor organizer Rafael Espinosa. Both Yang and Espinosa have deep East Side roots. They all agreed that the new library should emphasize its connection with the Civil Rights Movement, hence the adoption of the name "Freedom" Library.

The mission of the new organization was to contribute to the movement for social justice and equity by encouraging solidarity among working people, especially on the East Side. The ESFL would do this by collecting and preserving sources on labor, African-American, and immigration history, and by providing a welcoming space where people from diverse backgrounds could share their stories. Just as the St. Paul Public Library reinvented the public library by building branches in working-class neighborhoods in the early 20th century, now one of those Carnegie branches would be reinvented once again.

The newly formed non-profit led by Rachleff and Cleary entered into negotiations with the city to take over the building, supported by Ed Kodet, financial advisor Steve Boland, and lawyer Bob Long. Negotiations stalled because buying the building outright for

In 2014, the East Side Freedom Library opened in the former home of the Arlington Hills Public Library.

$365,000 was simply impossible. Council member Dan Bostrom broke the log jam by advocating for a lease, which, he said, would protect the interests of the city while allowing the East Side Freedom Library the opportunity to thrive and grow in the building.[12] In fact, only two other proposals had been received, neither of which met the city's conditions. Recognizing that the sale of the building at the asking price was not going to happen, the city council approved a $1 per year, fifteen-year lease on the condition that the ESFL fulfill several maintenance requirements, including a new roof.[13] The lease went into effect on June 1, 2014, and continues until 2029.

The city retained ownership of the building while the ESFL agreed to take on all responsibility not only for utility costs, but also for necessary maintenance and renovation.[14] The new roof, which turned out to cost about $60,000, was funded in part by a grant for more than $30,000 from the city's Neighborhood STAR Program. These tax-supported grants require a dollar for dollar match. The ESFL was able to quickly raise the matching funds through donations, mostly in small amounts by East Side neighbors.

Meanwhile, the new Arlington Hills Community Center opened at the corner of Payne and Maryland. The 41,000-square-foot building contained not only the new library but also a running track, fitness center, a teen multimedia lab, meeting rooms, classrooms, and a kitchen. At a ceremony in May 2014, Mayor Chris Coleman joined council member Dan Bostrom in celebrating the new building and the general renaissance of Payne Avenue after years of decay.[15]

The Arlington Hills Community Center, which houses the Arlington Hills Public Library.

Sources and Stories

Peter Rachleff retired from his position at Macalester College in the spring of 2014. Since then he has been the more-than-full-time volunteer director of the ESFL. Beth Cleary continues to work at Macalester but spends much of her free time at the library. They are assisted by a committed board and a small army of community members who participate in the work of the library by giving freely of their time. This dedicated team maintains regular hours, built a formidable research collection, organized an intense schedule of events, enhanced the exterior with attractive landscaping, completed numerous maintenance projects, created and managed a webpage and lively Facebook page, and has undertaken the constant fundraising work necessary to not only keep the doors open but also preserve and upgrade the historic building. In 2018, the ESFL had consolidated its financial base to the point where it was possible to hire Clarence White, an experienced writer, editor, and arts administrator, as their full-time Associate Director. The ESFL also formed a committed partnership with Marlin Heise, the curator of the Hmong Archives. These archives, now housed at ESFL, contain the premiere collection of Hmong books, documents, and materials in the world, and includes story cloths, musical instruments, and material objects.[16]

A story cloth from the Hmong Archives.

Under the leadership of Bruce Willms, retired dean of Metropolitan State University's library, 35 volunteers organized and cataloged over 20,000 books which provide rich coverage of labor, immigration, Africa-American, and social justice history. The volunteers have also created a fully-searchable online catalog of the collection (accessed from any computer at http://library.kohaesfl.org). The collection has been built through a series of gifts from the personal libraries of scholars, including the renowned labor historian David Montgomery, the musician and activist Fred Ho, and David Roediger, an influential historian of race and class.[17] The library has also benefited from the personal libraries of Minnesota-based scholars including Hy Berman, Sal Salerno, Paula Rabinowitz, Naomi Scheman, and of course, Peter Rachleff. The book collection quickly outgrew the shelf space of the former public library. John Sielaff, a "retired" carpenter and local historian, solved this problem by building three rows of shelving above each existing bookcase with lumber donated by ESFL supporters at Northern Forest Products.

David Montgomery

The collection operates as a research rather than a circulating library, meaning that researchers must use the books while in the library. Among the users of the collection are students from local middle and high schools who are preparing for the annual History Day competition. During the winter months, the library conducts History Day Learning Workshops every Saturday at which retired

A student hard at work on a History Day project at the library.

teachers, college students, and historians of all kinds work one-on-one with young people developing their projects. The library has also provided a place to showcase their completed projects. Many of their young scholars have won regional, state, and even national prizes.

The library has become a beehive of daily activity and scheduled events, many geared toward the creation and sharing of stories. Over 300 events attended by about 12,000 people were scheduled during the library's first four years. Some events are typical library fare, including authors like Brian McMahon talking about *The Ford Century in Minnesota,* his book about St. Paul's massive Ford assembly plant which closed in 2011, or the Saturday morning story hours for kids. There are also film showings, including a "Labor Movie Night," musical performances, theater productions, and poetry readings. For example, Rhythmic Literature, an Ethiopian poetry and art group dedicated to building solidarity among ethnic groups from Ethiopia and Eritrea, has used the library as its venue. The library also functions as a kind of union hall for the East Side community, with various labor organizations using the space for discussions, retreats, workshops, reading groups, and union job fairs. It's also a kind of clubhouse for various groups, including a Hmong women writers' group and a Karen women weavers' group. Perhaps the quintessential ESFL program is the monthly "Neighbors Meet

The Ethiopian group Rhythmic Literature performing at the East Side Freedom Library.

Neighbors" event at which representatives of one of the East Side's ethnic communities talk about their culture and experiences.

Like any new non-profit, the ESFL must work hard to meet its monthly expenses. In addition, the ESFL has the financial responsibilities that come with being a good steward of a historic building. Some of that work is done by volunteers, including Greg Poferl, a retired postal worker and high school teacher, who is a jack-of-all-trades. But maintaining and improving the building ultimately requires money, in significant amounts. Starting with the fundraising to match the STAR grant that funded the new roof, the library has developed a broad base of individual supporters. The ESFL has also received support from the St. Paul Regional Labor Federation and other labor organizations, and grants from various sources including the St. Paul Foundation, the Minnesota Historical and Cultural Grants program (popularly known as "Legacy grants"), the John S. and James L. Knight Foundation, and other foundations. Bigger funding challenges are quickly approaching, including the replacement of the building's aging heating and air conditioning system and the repair of the exterior stone and brickwork. The ESFL team also has a renovation wish list, from a new floor in the downstairs auditorium to a real kitchen, both of which would make the building more suitable for its new uses. Future budgets will have to provide for the hiring of more staff as the project grows and the founding directors retire.

In any case, the ESFL has gotten off to a strong start and, over its first five years, has made great progress towards fulfilling its goals. In recognition of this progress, the American Library Association chose the ESFL to be the recipient of the John Sessions Memorial Award, which recognizes a library which has made a significant effort to work with the labor community in order to heighten awareness of "the history and contribution of the labor movement to the development of the United States."[18] The East Side Area Business Association gave the library its "Commitment to the Community Award" in 2017, and the library also received a 2017 "Arts Achievement Award" from the Metropolitan Regional Arts Council.

In 2017, the St. Paul Public Library celebrated the centennial of the St. Anthony Park, Riverview, and Arlington Hills branches as well as its main building on Rice Park. The ESFL joined in this commemoration of the 100th anniversary of Andrew Carnegie's gift to the city not only because it occupies one of these historic buildings, but also because it feels a strong bond between the building of an impressive branch library for the immigrant communities of the East Side a century ago and the creation of a new kind of library for those communities today.

This sense of historical continuity was dramatized in 2014 at the ESFL's first major event, a celebration of the African American holiday, Juneteenth, which marks the coming of freedom to the last enslaved people in the South in June of 1865. The evening featured a dramatic reading of Frederick Douglass' famous speech "What to the Slave is the Fourth of July?" In the first chapter of this book, we saw that Frederick Douglass spoke in Minnesota several times in the years after the Civil War, often invited by local library associations who raised funds by sponsoring lectures. The St. Paul Library Association, for example, benefitted from his sold-out lecture in 1869. At the Juneteenth event in 2014, historian Mahmoud El-Kati introduced Douglass' speech as performed by actor Andre Samples, University of Minnesota professor John Wright, and actor and playwright Taous Claire Khazem.[19]

Douglass delivered his speech on July 5, 1852, at the Corinthian Hall in Rochester, New York, where he lived at the time. Douglass

Corinthian Hall at Rochester, New York.

insisted on this date because he did not want to celebrate the Fourth of July holiday, honoring a local practice among African Americans in the state of New York. Corinthian Hall was a classically designed space established in part by the Mechanics Literary Association, which was founded in 1830 by a group of young artisans who called themselves "the meddling class." Its interior had tall ceilings and rows of windows, not much different than the interior of the East Side Freedom Library. The hall hosted Charles Dickens, Susan B. Anthony, Ralph Waldo Emerson, and other great lecturers of the time, among whom Douglass was perhaps the most dynamic. In his speech, Douglass noted the "scorching irony" of the Fourth of July, which more than anything only reminds the Negro population of "the gross injustice and cruelty" of slavery.[20]

Since that opening program, the ESFL has continued to investigate, celebrate, and promote freedom. Like the Corinthian Hall, the ESFL has developed into a thriving "free space," the kind of place where the public good is discussed and nurtured. It is a lively reinvention of the branch library built with Carnegie funds in Arlington Heights. The neighborhood still has its public library, now housed in the Arlington Hills Community Center a few blocks away on Payne. The East Side Freedom Library has reinvented the original Carnegie building into a new kind of library and community space. The two libraries together are part of the ongoing renaissance of the East Side.

We live in times when the daily news can quickly deflate your spirit. But all around us, people are digging in for the long haul and building organizations and institutions which will carry us forward. The East Side Freedom Library has established itself as one of those places where the future is being created on a strong foundation of the past. "Free spaces" like this give us every reason to be hopeful about the future. They deserve our support and participation.

A Closer Look....

A Mural of East Side Immigration History

The stairway mural.

The East Side Freedom Library is about telling stories in many forms, one of which is a mural in the stairway linking the main level to the basement. Funded with a grant from the John S. and James L. Knight Foundation, the library commissioned Hmong artist Ger (Jackie) Yang to create a mural depicting the immigration history of the East

Side. Yang began developing his artistic skills as a refugee in Thailand. His murals can be seen at such places as the Hmong Village shopping center and the Roseville Adult Learning Center.

As you descend the stairway, you follow a timeline of Minnesota history, starting with the Dakota, and moving on to the European-Americans, African-Americans, and the more recent Latino and Southeast Asian immigrant communities, including, of course, the Hmong. To help Yang create the images for the mural, Peter Rachleff arranged meetings between Yang and various groups, including Native Americans, Latinos, and Karen. They brought ideas, and in some cases, contributed images to the mural.

A portion of the mural depicting the traditional Hmong life in the Laotian highlands.

- Chapter 5 Endnotes -

[1] Jason Hoppin, "Libraries Propose $57 M Makeover—Plan Includes New East Side Library. *St. Paul Pioneer Press,* June 21, 2007. B3. Holzman Moss Architecture, LLP, "St. Paul Public Library: Branch Programming Study," (May 2007). It seems clear that the decision to replace the Arlington Hills Public Library with a community center shared by the library and a recreation center had been made prior to the report. The report does not recommend this result, but assumes it to be a fact.

[2] Daniel B. Bostrom, Ward News, March 2008. *The Payne Maryland Neighborhood Vision Statement,* July 2008 (available on the St. Paul Park and Recreation webpage).

[3] Interview with Ward Six Council Member Don Bostrom at his office in the St. Paul City Hall on September 6, 2017.

[4] Although the hardware store was at first reluctant to move, the new location turned out to be profitable. Frederick Melo, "St. Paul: Kendall's hardware celebrates successful first year," *St. Paul Pioneer Press,* October 10. 2013.

[5] Frederick Melo, "Payne-Maryland project in St. Paul loses a partner, *St. Paul Pioneer Press,* February 10, 2011.

[6] Frederick Melo, "Library/Recreation center plans critiqued—Public offers views of multifaceted 'Town Square' plan," *St. Paul Pioneer Press,* August 25, 2011, p. B1.

[7] Frederick Melo, "Payne-Phalen 'Super-center' revised to please neighbors—Construction to start this summer," *St. Paul Pioneer Press,* February 22, 2011, p. B3.

[8] Frederick Melo, "Sale of one of city's oldest libraries approved," *St. Paul Pioneer Press,* July 11, 2013, p. A8.

[9] "For Sale: Arlington Hills Library." This is an 11-page full color listing document providing potential buyers with information about the building. Thanks to Bruce Engelbrekt, Real Estate Manager, Office of Financial Services and Real Estate, City of St. Paul for sharing this document and providing background on the proposed sale of the library.

[10] Kevin Clemens, *Carnegie Libraries of Minnesota* (Lake Elmo, MN: Demontreville Press, Inc, 2011).

[11] Frederick Melo, "Sale of one of city's oldest libraries approved," *St. Paul Pioneer Press,* July 13, 2012, p. A8; Jim Anderson, "For Sale: Landmark Library," *Minneapolis Star Tribune,* October 11, 2013, p. B1, B5.

[12] Interview with Ward Six Council Member Don Bostrom at his office in the St. Paul City Hall on September 6, 2017.

[13] Frederick Melo, "East Side: Old Library, leased by city, to house labor collection," *St. Paul Pioneer Press,* March 20, 2014, p. A7.

[14] Interview with Bruce Engelbrekt in his office at the St. Paul City Annex on September 6, 2017.

[15] Frederick Melo, "Arlington Hills library/rec center gives East Side a boost—41,000 square-foot project finally complete," *St. Paul Pioneer Press*, May 23, 2014, p. A7.

[16] The Hmong Archives is an independent non-profit established in the 1990s by Marlin Heise, an archivist at the Minnesota Historical Society, and Yuepheng Xiong, a bookstore owner and community activist who emigrated from Laos with his parents in 1979. In addition to books, the archives collect artifacts including "story cloths," tools, household items, and musical instruments. This growing collection was housed in various places until relocating to the ESFL in 2016. Heise, now retired from MHS, sits on the board of the ESFL

[17] David Montgomery (1927–2011) was a machinist and union organizer in St. Paul before he earned his Ph.D in labor history at the University of Minnesota. He went on to transform the study of American labor history while teaching at a number of universities. His classic work is *The Fall of the House of Labor.* Peter Rachleff studied with Montgomery while earning his Ph.D. at the University of Pittsburgh. Fred Ho (1957–2014) was a composer, saxophonist, writer, and activist who composed politically charged operas, suites, oratorios, and ballets that mixed jazz with popular and traditional elements of what he called Afro-Asian culture. Among David Roediger's many books is *The Wages of Whiteness: Race and the Making of the American Working Class*. He taught at the University of Minnesota in the late 1990s and today teaches at the University of Kansas.

[18] "East Side Freedom Library wins major award for partnership with unions," *The St. Paul Union Advocate*, April 15, 2017, p. 8.

[19] Andy Sturdevant, "'The Meddling class' finds its righteous voice at East Side Freedom Library," *MinnPost*, July 10, 2014.

[20] In an appendix to his autobiography *My Bondage and My Freedom*, Douglass included an excerpt from the speech under the title "What to the Slave is the Fourth of July." Frederick Douglass, *Autobiographies* (New York: The Library of America, 1994). The speech sometimes appears under the title "The Meaning of July Fourth for the Negro," as in Howard Zinn and Anthony Arnove, *Voices of a People's History of the United States* (New York: Seven Stories Press, 2004).

- Bibliography -

Baldwin, Clara F. "The Public Library Movement in Minnesota, 1900–1936." *Minnesota Libraries.* December, 1945, 384–398.

Benidt, Bruce Weir. *The Library Book: A Centennial History of the Minneapolis Public Library.* Minneapolis: Minneapolis Public Library, 1984.

Blight, David W. *Frederick Douglass: Prophet of Freedom.* New York: Simon & Schuster, 2018.

Bobinski, George S. *Carnegie Libraries: Their History and Impact on American Public Library Development.* Chicago: American Library Association, 1969.

Bostwick, Arthur E. *The American Public Library.* 4th Ed. New York: D. Appleton and Company, 1929.

Breisch, Kenneth A. *American Libraries 1730–1950.* New York: W. W. Norton, 2017.

Carlstedt, Ellworth. "The Public Library Movement in Minnesota, 1849–1900." *Minnesota Libraries,* September 1945, p. 351–363.

Carnegie, Andrew. *Autobiography of Andrew Carnegie.* Boston: Houghton Mifflin, 1920.

Carnegie, Andrew. *The Gospel of Wealth, and Other Timely Essays.* Cambridge, MA: Belknap Press of Harvard University Press, 1962.

Castle, Henry A. *History of St. Paul and Vicinity.* 3 vols. Chicago: Lewis Publishing Co., 1912.

Cherry, DeAnne Marie. "Growing Up in St. Paul: A Stroll Down Memory Lane: Payne Avenue in the 1950s," *Ramsey County History,* Vol, 38, No 3 (Fall 2003): 22–25.

Chrislock, Carl. *The Progressive Era in Minnesota.* St. Paul: Minnesota Historical Society Press, 1971.

Chrislock, Carl. *Watchdog of Loyalty: the Minnesota Commission of Public Safety During World War I.* St. Paul: Minnesota Historical Society Press, 1991.

Clemens, Kevin. *Carnegie Libraries of Minnesota.* Lake Elmo, MN: Demontreville Press, Inc., 2011.

Denning, Michael. *Mechanic Accents: Dime Novels and Working-Class Culture in America.* New York: Verso, 1987.

Foner, Philip S. *Frederick Douglass.* New York: International Publishers, 1964.

Foner, Philip S. and Robert Branhan. *Lift Every Voice: African-American Oratory 1787–1900.* Tuscaloosa: University of Alabama Press, 1998.

Freeze, Lauren. "St. Paul's Beaux-Arts Carnegie Libraries: Philanthropic Architecture in a Local Context." *Ramsey County History* 47, No. 1 (Spring 2016): 3–12.

Garland, Robert F. "The Other Librarian: Clara Baldwin and the Public Library Movement in Minnesota," *Ramsey County History* 42, No 3 (Fall, 2007): 4–10.

Gaut, Greg. *Laird's Legacy: A History of the Winona Public Library.* Winona: Friends of the Winona Public Library, 2016.

Hess, Jeffrey and Paul Larson. *St. Paul Architecture: A History.* Minneapolis: University of Minnesota Press, 2006.

Jones, Theodore. *Carnegie Libraries Across America: A Public Legacy.* New York: John Wiley, 1997.

Lanegran, David A. "Swedish Neighborhoods of the Twin Cities: From Swede Hollow to Arlington Heights, From Snoose Boulevard to Minnehaha Parkway," in Philip J. Anderson and Dag Blanck, *Swedes in the Twin Cities.* St. Paul: Minnesota Historical Society Press, 2001.

Lansing, Michael J. *Insurgent Democracy: The Nonpartisan League in North American Politics.* Chicago: University of Chicago Press, 2015.

League of Women Voters of Minnesota. *Funding of Public Libraries in Minnesota.* November, 1978.

Miller, Durand R. *Carnegie Grants for Library Buildings 1890–1917.* New York: Carnegie Corporation, 1943.

Millett, Larry. *AIA Guide to the Twin Cities.* St. Paul: Minnesota Historical Society Press, 2007.

Millett, Larry. *Lost Twin Cities.* St. Paul: Minnesota Historical Society Press, 1992.

Murphy, Patricia et al. "St. Anthony Park, Arlington Hills, and Riverview Carnegie Libraries." *National Register of Historic Places Inventory-Nomination Form,* November 12, 1981.

Nasaw, David. *Andrew Carnegie.* New York: Penguin, 2006.

Office of the Legislative Auditor, Program Evaluation Division. *Public Libraries: Evaluation Report.* St. Paul: Office of the Legislative Auditor, March 2010.

Ohman, Doug. *Libraries of Minnesota.* St. Paul, MN: Minnesota Historical Society Press, 2011.

Ostendorf, Paul J. *The History of the Public Library Movement in Minnesota from 1849 to 1916.* Ph.D dissertation. University of Minnesota, 1984.

Pawley, Christine. *Libraries and the Reading Public in Twentieth-Century America.* Madison, Wisconsin: The University of Wisconsin Press, 2013.

Pejsa, Jane. *Gratia Countryman: Her Life, Her Loves, and Her Library.* Minneapolis: Nodin Press, 1995.

Phelps, Gary. "The St. Paul Library and Its First 100 Years." *Ramsey County History* 18, No. 1 (1982): 3–23.

Regan, Ann. "The Irish" in June Drenning Holmquist. *They Chose Minnesota: A Survey of the State's Ethnic Group.* St. Paul: Minnesota Historical Society Press, 1981.

Sielaff, John. "Nels Nelson—Master Stonemason," *Who Built Our Capitol* website (https://www.whobuiltourcapitol.org/).

Trimble, Steve. "From the Land of Sky Blue Waters," *Saint Paul Historical,* accessed September 25, 2017, http://saintpaulhistorical.com/items/show/1.

Valdes, Dennis. *Barrios Nortenos: St. Paul and Midwestern Mexican Communities in the Twentieth Century.* Austin: University of Texas Press, 2000.

Van Slyck, Abigail A. *Free to All: Carnegie Libraries and American Culture 1890–1920.* Chicago: University of Chicago Press, 1995.

Vang, Chia Youyee. *Hmong in Minnesota.* St. Paul: Minnesota Historical Society Press, 2008.

Vang, Chia Youyee. *Hmong America: Reconstructing Community in Diaspora.* Urbana: University of Illinois Press, 2010.

Vecoli, Rudi. "The Italians," in June Drenning Holmquist. *They Chose Minnesota: A Survey of the State's Ethnic Group.* St. Paul: Minnesota Historical Society Press, 1981.

Westerberg, Kermit B. "Libraries, Immigrants, Communities," in Philip Anderson and Dag Blanck, *Swedes in the Twin Cities.* St. Paul: Minnesota Historical Society Press, 2001.

Wiegand, Wayne A. *Main Street Public Library: Community Places and Reading Spaces in the Rural Heartland, 1876–1956.* Iowa City: University of Iowa Press, 2011.

Wiegand, Wayne A. *Part of Our Lives: A People's History of the American Public Library.* New York: Oxford U. Press, 2015.

Yang, Kao Kalia. "Invisible Stories," pp 111–117 in Doug Ohman, *Libraries of Minnesota.* St. Paul: Minnesota Historical Society, 2011.

Young, Biloine W. *A Noble Task: The Saint Paul Public Library Celebrates 125!* Afton, MN: Afton Historical Society Press, 2007.

- Acknowledgments -

This book was made possible by two grants from the Minnesota Arts and Cultural Heritage Fund administered by the Minnesota Historical Society. This fund was created in 2008 when Minnesota voters passed the Clean Water, Land, and Legacy constitutional amendment. Thanks very much to those voters!

These St. Paul librarians, most of whom worked at either the old or new Arlington Hills branch, helped with sources and background: Karen Kolb Peterson, Tracy Baumann, Mary Margaret Sullivan, Dua Thao, Buddy Ferrari, Lora Bloom, Peter Borgen, and Barbara Malas. Thanks to each of you.

Several years ago, the St. Paul Public Library gave 37 boxes of records to the State Archives of the Minnesota Historical Society. Even though they were in the process of cataloging these materials, archivists Charles Rogers and Anjanette Schlusser provided me with comfortable access. I appreciated their hospitality. Across the river, Ted Hathaway and Baily Diers at the Hennepin County Public Library Special Collections at Minneapolis Central were helpful as always.

I valued the opportunity to interview former St. Paul City Council Member Dan Bostrom about the process that led to the new Arlington Hills Public Library. Thanks also to Scott Renstrom for arranging the interview. Bruce Engelbrekt, real estate manager in the city's Office of Financial Services, helped me understand the process that led to the lease of the Carnegie building to the East Side Freedom Library. His colleague Barbara Morin alerted me to the existence of Charles Hausler's original plans to the Arlington Hills Library and graciously provided digital copies.

Yuichiro Onishi, a board member at the East Side Freedom Library, provided me with an invaluable set of copies of correspondence between the St. Paul Public Library and the Carnegie Corporation officials in New York. Thanks also to local historians John Sielaff and Dave Riehle for providing crucial sources on local labor history, and to Steve Trimble for contributing his piece on

Swede Hollow. Steve Wandler shared his research on Frederick Douglass's visits to Minnesota. I learned much from architect Ed Kodet's presentation on the architecture of the Arlington Hills Public Library.

The historians Annette Atkins, Professor Emeritus at St. John's University and Michael Lansing, Associate Professor at Augsburg College gave the initial draft a close reading and shared many helpful insights which were a great help.

It has been a pleasure working with Wendy Johnson, doing business as Elder Eye Press and Design, who copy edited and designed the book. Thanks also to mapmaker Nat Case for the historic East Side map. Special thanks to East Side Freedom Library collaborators A. J. Decker and Emma Niemaszyk for their work creating the index. In the production phase, the book benefited from the experience of Tom O'Connell, Peter Rachleff, and Clarence White.

Finally, thanks to Beth Cleary and Peter Rachleff for sharing their story, and to Peter for providing many insights into the labor and immigration history of St. Paul. I joined in one of his walking tours up Payne Avenue from Swede Hollow, and my wife Marsha Neff and I have enjoyed our own historic explorations of the East Side.

- Image Credits -

- Cover -

Photograph – by Steve Boland.

- Chapter One -

All photographs, except on page 21 – courtesy of the Minnesota Historical Society.

Photograph, page 21 – public domain.

- Chapter Two -

Photographs, pages 29, 34 – public domain.

Photographs, pages 36, 39, 40, 47, and 49 – courtesy of the Minnesota Historical Society.

Architectural plans, pages 42, 43, 45 – courtesy of the City of St. Paul.

Photograph, page 45 – courtesy of the St. Paul Public Library.

- Chapter Three -

All photographs, except on pages 57 and 59 – courtesy of the Minnesota Historical Society.

Photograph, page 57 – by Greg Gaut.

Photograph, page 59 – public domain.

Map illustration, page 65 – Nat Case of INCase, LLC.

- Chapter Four -

Photographs, pages 80, 88 – courtesy of the Minnesota Historical Society.

Photograph, page 82 – by Caleb Williams, Creative Commons license.

Photographs, pages 83, 93 – by Greg Gaut.

Photograph, page 84 – public domain.

Photographs, pages 86, 96 – courtesy of the St. Paul Public Library.

Photograph, page 92 – courtesy of Kao Kalia Yang.

- Chapter Five -

Photograph, page 102 – courtesy of Dan Bostrom.

Photograph, page 105 – by Steve Boland.

Photograph page 106 – courtesy of Hatch-Billops Collections.

Photographs, pages 108, 109, 116, 117 – by Greg Gaut.

Photograph, page 110, story cloth – courtesy of the Hmong Archives.

Photograph, page 110, David Montgomery – courtesy of the Labor and Working-Class History Association.

Photograph page 111 – by Greg Poferl.

Photograph page 112 – by Kal Molla.

Photograph, page 114 – public domain.

- Index -

C

D

E

F

G

H

I

J

K

L

M

O

P

R

S

T

U

V

W

Y

46988240R00086

Made in the USA
Middletown, DE
04 June 2019